Don't Pay Too Much Tax If You're Self-Employed

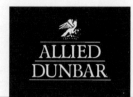

ALLIED
DUNBAR

PERSONAL FINANCE GUIDES

In the same series:

Running Your Own Business
(Third Edition)
David Williams

Don't Pay Too Much Tax If You're Self-Employed

David Williams

NICHOLAS BREALEY
PUBLISHING

LONDON

First published in Great Britain by
Nicholas Brealey Publishing Limited in 1994
21 Bloomsbury Way
London WC1A 2TH

© Allied Dunbar Assurance plc, 1994

ISBN 1-85788-091-9

British Library Cataloguing-in-Publication Data
A catalogue record for this book is available from the British Library

Typeset by Frere Publishing Services, 2 Whitehorse Street, London W1
Printed and bound in Great Britain by Biddles Ltd

Contents

Acknowledgements

I owe thanks to many people who helped bring this book into being with examples and ideas, including colleagues and students and in the early stages, my late father. David Vessey of Allied Dunbar, Nick Brealey and Rupert Scott helped considerably with the production of this edition. As ever, Lis, Edward and Tom (and Richard at a distance) helped, each in their own way! But the book and its approach are mine.

As with all tax books, this will date as fast as governments change their minds. However, the text takes account of the Finance Act 1994 and all changes prior to that time.

D. Williams

May 1994.

Introduction

In the last two years, something of a myth has been destroyed in Britain. It is the myth that governments can cut taxes to the point that they no longer matter. Many governments of many persuasions in many countries have tried this but all they succeed in doing is cutting some of the taxes on some of the people for some of the time. To misquote Abraham Lincoln, you can cut taxes for some of the people for some of the time, but you cannot cut taxes on all of the people for all the time.

For the next few years, taxes are going to rise for most people. That is why it is important to understand them and how they affect your business. This book is written to get you thinking about this. Its aim is to introduce all the taxes that will affect your business. Hopefully, by understanding what is going on, you can ensure that you pay only the taxes due from you. Remember...you owe it to yourself to understand your taxes. If not, you will probably owe them to someone else.

Ever had one of these?

Inland Revenue
Notice to Pay

C
D

INCOME TAX
YEAR 1993-94

Reference number	File number
661 DG 61067 9201	

TAX £   **10,000.00**

Date   **02 DEC 1991**

Mr A. N. Other

100 ACACIA AVENUE
ANYTOWN
N1Y 7LA

Application is made for payment of the amount shown on the attached payslip.

You are reminded that interest is chargeable on tax paid late (see notes overleaf).

Cashier's stamp and initials

- **How to pay:** *See overleaf.*

- **Please write the Reference number shown above on the back of your cheque.**

Collector of Taxes
Inland Revenue Accounts Office (Shipley)
BRADFORD
West Yorkshire BD98 8AA
Telephone: Bradford (0274) 594141

Gi Girobank *Trans cash*
Girobank plc Bootle Merseyside GIR 0AA

Payslip

Bank Giro Credit

Reference number

158 208	661DG610679201	1

Credit account number

610 5041

AMOUNT DUE
(No fee payable at PO counter)

£   **10,000.00**

By transfer from Girobank account no.

Cashier's stamp and initials

Signature ....
Date ....

Mr A.N. Other

For official use only

10 - 50 - 41

BANK OF ENGLAND
HEAD OFFICE COLLECTION A/C
INLAND REVENUE

Cash

Cheques

£

Items   Fee paid

DN1(Z)

Please do not fold this payslip or write or mark below this line.

661DG000610679201E   &7006105041   000301256   74   X

1 *Taxes you don't - and do - have to pay*

*T*AX DEMANDS are good news and bad news. They are good news if they show you earn a healthy profit from your business, and they ask you to pay no more than the proper amount of tax. Many are bad news, and not just because they demand money. People haven't planned to pay the bill and cannot afford it, or haven't the records to check if they are asked to pay too much, or don't know enough about taxation to know what the bill is about.

IS IT GOOD NEWS OR BAD NEWS?

If you thought tax was bad news in the last few years, then the bad news is really coming! Between the tax year 1992-93 and the tax year 1996-97, total tax bills are going to rise on present plans by £15,000,000,000 or more - that is, about £5 a week for every individual in the land, old and young, earners and non-earners, you and me. In practice, that means that each taxpayer is going to have to pay considerably more. What is more, current predictions show that taxes will rise even further after that.

Tax is often a big worry to the self-employed and equally to investors living from a combined use of their savings and their skills (as landlords do). It is - and should be - a major concern to those who have a second income from self-employment besides the `day job'. It can be complicated dealing with the competing demands of income tax, capital gains tax, NI contributions, VAT, ...

THE AIMS OF THIS BOOK

That's where this book comes in. Its purpose is threefold. It works with you to take the unnecessary worry out of tax. It does so by showing you what you need to do to comply with the requirements of tax officials. It explains the reasons behind some of the tax rules. And it helps you set about planning your tax affairs so you pay no more tax than you should and no sooner than you should.

Some people respond to the pressures of the tax system by ignoring or evading the taxes. That is increasingly hard to do. The penalties for evading tax are much stiffer than they were - ask anyone caught out for not complying with the VAT laws recently. Others hand their tax affairs over to someone else to do, without asking any questions. Sometimes they later regret it. As others will also tell you, handing over your VAT forms to an incompetent accountant does not stop you being responsible for the errors - and penalties. We look at when you need - and when you do not need - help in the next chapter. Many others just fill in the forms and pay the tax bills without question, assuming the tax authority must be right. Perhaps they should be - but one survey not long ago found that as many as one in four of all tax computations by the Inland Revenue was wrong! If you do not give them the right information, it may not be their fault they are wrong.

What we do in this book is to look at the aspects of your business that are liable to tax (well, let's be honest at the start - <u>all</u> aspects of your business are liable to tax, so we will look at all of them). We see what taxes are involved and how to set about handling them. The aims in each case are to show you how the system works, and how to make sure it is working fairly on your business.

Tax officials and tax advisers love jargon (just like the rest of us). They'll talk about Schedules and tax points, rollover reliefs and golden handcuffs, categorisation and top-slicing ... In this book we try to get the junk element out of what is said. It is impossible to do so entirely, because you need to know some of the jargon, too. To help avoid confusion, there is a list of technical words and jargon at the end of the book, and words defined in that list are put in **bold type** to show that the word is in the list. My job is to cut out the jargon, but yours is ...

CUTTING OUT THE
JARGON

Set about your tax affairs with the aim of complying with your legal obligations. At the same time, use your rights under the law to pay only the tax that is properly due after all allowances and deductions. Important rules allow you to reduce or postpone - and sometimes entirely to remove - your tax

CUTTING OUT
THE TAXES

liabilities. But it is for you to claim most of these deductions. You won't get them automatically. How do you set about doing this? First, some `dos' and `don'ts'.

TAX DOS AND DON'TS:

Do take sensible steps to avoid unnecessary taxation, but don't try to reduce your tax bill by evasion.

Do find out what deductions you can claim, but don't get carried away into spending money just to save tax.

Do allow for tax when planning your business, but don't let tax considerations dominate all you do.

Do look to the future for your family and for your own retirement, and don't think it won't happen to you - sooner or later it will.

Do keep all appropriate books and records for your tax accounts; don't expect the tax inspector to believe you won all your money, or were left it by Great Aunt Agatha unless you have kept the proof.

Do consider appointing a tax adviser to deal with your tax affairs, but don't use the fact that you have an adviser as an excuse to ignore your tax affairs yourself.

Tax departments can only collect tax from you if they have the clear authority of Parliament to do so. Centuries of our constitutional history and several revolutions have - just about - established that. (If you want to learn something of tax history, borrow a copy of C.Northcote Parkinson's *The Law and the Profits* from somewhere - it will tell you all you need to know.) That is of immense practical importance, because it means <u>they</u> can only require <u>you</u> to pay up if they can show Parliament has ordered you to do so. Before you leap up and down at this ray of hope, be warned - it is safe to say that Parliament has ordered most people to pay tax on most things. But not everything, which is why we need to watch carefully what is and what is not covered.

THE AUTHORITY TO TAX

The key point is that both you and the tax departments must follow the rules. From that flow two fundamental principles :

BASIC PRINCIPLES OF TAXING

That the tax authorities cannot impose a tax unless the law makes it clear that the tax is properly authorised

That taxpayers cannot escape tax, or ask for deductions, unless they show clear legal authority for that escape or deduction

These principles prevent tax authorities operating by whim, but do not avoid all disputes. They and you may not agree what the rules say. A third principle applies if that occurs. **You have the right to have disputes decided by impartial judges** in tax tribunals and the courts. Having said that, it is far better to sort out most disputes by negotiation if you can.

A fourth principle follows from these three. **You are entitled to conduct your tax affairs in any way that you wish, unless the tax authorities can show clear authority for requiring you to deal with matters in a certain way.** If you can deal with something in two ways, one of which results in you paying less tax or paying tax later, it is your choice which way you handle the matter. We call this tax avoidance, or tax planning, much of which is plainly common sense.

Some of these points - and others - are set out in the **Taxpayer's Charter**, which all tax departments take very seriously. There are also **Contributor's Charters** for NI contributions.

THE TAXPAYER'S CHARTER

You are entitled to expect the Inland Revenue

To be fair
- By settling your tax affairs impartially
- By expecting you to pay only what is due under the law
- By treating everyone with equal fairness

To help you
- To get you tax affairs right
- To understand your rights and obligations
- By providing clear leaflets and forms
- By giving you information and assistance at our enquiry offices
- By being courteous at all times

To provide an efficient service
- By settling your tax affairs promptly and accurately
- By keeping you private affairs strictly confidential
- By using the information give us only as allowed by the law
- By keeping to a minimum your costs of complying with the law
- By keeping our costs down

To be accountable for what we do
- By setting standards for ourselves and publishing how well we live up to them

If you are not satisfied
- We will tell you exactly how to complain
- You can ask for tax affairs to be looked at again
- You can appeal to an independent tribunal
- Your MP can refer your complaint to the Ombudsman

In return, we need you
- To be honest
- To give us accurate information
- To pay your tax on time

IT'S TOO DIFFICULT FOR ME TO UNDERSTAND

That's what many people say about their tax affairs. Many are wrong. The basic principles of all our taxes are extremely simple. The trouble lies in the detail.

Because of over a century of `us and them' disputes, the simple frameworks of our taxes have been overlaid by complicated specific provisions dealing with particular problems. These are frequently written in some of the worst forms of official English you can find anywhere. One reason for this is an attempt to make the sections lawyer-proof. The draftsmen know that every word of every rule gets pecked and scratched at by tax experts with the same thoroughness that owners of chickens will recognise when their hens are hunting for an insect or worm. And, as fowl owners will also know, the result is that what ought to be the vegetable garden gets turned into a mess. They are always hunting for the foodstuffs to produce a golden egg.

This detail is important in practice, but it should not obscure (as it frequently does) the underlying rules, which are really rather straightforward. This book concentrates on those principles, and their practical consequences. That is how the great majority of tax matters are decided. Don't be put off - you can understand it. Then you won't pay too much.

TYPES OF INCOME

You will be involved, as an unpaid collector of taxes, with several taxes. The best way to summarise what you need to watch is by referring to different kinds of income or transactions:

Trading income

This is taxed in three ways at once:

> There is an income tax charge on your net profits from the trade, that is, on the income less the expenses.   This is called Schedule D Case I (its official name in tax law).
>
> There is an NI contributions charge on the net profits, backed by a flat rate levy on all the self-employed.
>
> There is value added tax (VAT) on each VATable supply of goods or services made by the trade.

If a company runs the trade, it will not pay income tax. Instead it pays **corporation tax** on the profits. Companies do not pay NI contributions except for their employees.

Professional income

Tax, eg, on architects and artists, is levied in the same three ways as trading income, but is called **Schedule D Case II.**

Gains from selling capital items

Selling capital items that are used in a business (eg a shop or land) is treated the same way for tax purposes as selling private assets (such as a valuable painting). In either case, the individual may be liable for a **capital gains tax** charge on the profits from the sale. A company making a gain does not pay CGT, but a charge to **corporation tax** on a chargeable gain. If the seller is in business, he, she or it will also probably have to charge **VAT** on making the sale. If selling land or shares, you will have to pay a third tax, **stamp duty**.

Exports and imports
Whilst profits on exports and imports are the same for income tax purposes as goods bought or sold in the UK, the VAT rules are entirely different. If you are exporting goods to a country outside the European Union, or importing goods from outside, you must watch **customs duties** when you import goods.

Income from overseas
This is dealt with by separate rules from those applying to income from inside the UK (and covered by **Schedule D Cases IV and V**). If you have little connection with the UK, there will be no, or reduced, liability to tax. This book concentrates (as do most others) on the rules that operate here, so this is an extra reason to seek advice.

Rents, etc, from land
Landlords pay income tax on rents from land under a different set of rules to those applying to trading income. This is known as **Schedule A**. NI contributions do not apply to a landlord's income from land. VAT is not usually payable on rent.

Using land
It may sound odd that you are taxed on using land, but that is how **business rates** work. It is assumed that you are paying rent on your land (even if you are not), and the amount of rates is based on this rent. For individuals, there is the new local **council tax** to pay on their homes.

Dividends from companies
Individuals receiving dividends and other

distributions from companies in the UK pay income tax on them - though the company has invariably paid this for you. The income tax rules for this differ from trading income rules and are known as **Schedule F**. Companies receiving these payments do not pay any further tax. There is no VAT on dividends.

Interest

The rules for taxing interest are rather messy. Normally income tax (or, for companies, corporation tax) on long-term loans is payable under another set of rules, **Schedule D Case III.** There is no good reason for this, and the government is reviewing these rules. Other rules apply to some forms of government stock, and some forms (like National Savings) are not liable to tax at all. VAT is not charged on interest.

Earnings from employment

These are liable to two taxes: *income tax* under another set of income tax rules   (**Schedule E**), and *NI contributions* payable both by employee and employer.

Pensions

Whether paid by the employer, the state, or personal pension or private scheme, these are treated in the same way as earnings. Some social security payments, like retirement pensions, are liable to tax. Others are not.

Prizes and winnings

Most prizes and winnings are free of tax (except the special taxes on betting, football pools and so forth). Prizes won from professional competitions may be treated as professional or trading income.

Gifts and bequests

These do not get caught by income tax (unless

they are a disguised form of earnings). They may get caught for: *capital gains tax* as if there had been a sale (this can be postponed, as shown below). There is no CGT payable when someone leaves property to someone else on death; nor is there **inheritance tax**, if the gift is large and occurs within 7 years of the giver's death.

Grants
Most grants are liable to income tax, though some are tax free. Grants from private sources are sometimes treated as gifts or prizes.

Increased value of unsold items
The fact that your assets, such as the items used for your business, go up in value during the year does not affect your tax position. We have no **wealth tax** on property we own. The one exception to this is **trading stock**. The value of trading stock is taken into account in working out trading profits for income tax or corporation tax.

TYPES OF TAX

You may find it useful to have that information summarised tax by tax. You need mostly to think about - and probably pay - the following:

Income tax - on trading profits, rents, professional income, bank interest, dividends, other savings interest and earnings from employment.

Business rates - on use of all business premises, payable to the local council.

Capital gains tax (almost always called **CGT**) - on any gain you make when disposing (whether by sale, exchange, gift or otherwise) of any kind of property. It applies where the gain is not regarded as trading income.

Council tax - payable by individuals to the councils of the areas where they live. It replaces the domestic rates and the poll tax.

Corporation tax - paid by companies instead of income tax and CGT; its rules are much the same as IT and CGT.

Customs duty - on any goods you import from outside the **European Economic Area (EEA)**, but not on items you get, say, from France or Sweden. Similarly, if you export to countries outside the EEA, your goods will probably be subject to customs duty as they enter the importing country.

Inheritance tax (IHT) - is really two taxes in one: a tax on property left by someone at death, and a tax on gifts made within 7 years before death. It only affects large sums, but is important in long-term planning.

NI contributions - all self-employed people, like all employees - must pay NI contributions out of their earnings.

Stamp duty - payable when you buy or lease land or buy shares or stock. It is a levy on the value of the land or shares changing hands.

Value added tax (called, here as everywhere else, VAT) - tax on all supplies of goods and services made by businesses.

These aren't all the UK taxes. There are **excise duties** levied on tobacco, petrol, beer, wine and spirits, betting and gambling, insurance policies, the gas levy, even air tickets, which have to be paid. Costly as these are, they are specific taxes paid by producers or importers, or by those needing licences to keep, say, gaming machines. These are mentioned where appropriate in the book - and there are other taxes, varying from petroleum revenue tax to gun licences, which we ignore because they won't affect your business (unless you are in the oil industry or run a hunt for profit).

The difference between avoidance and evasion of taxes is fundamental. **Evasion** means cutting tax bills illegally - by making sure the tax office have never heard of you (**ghosting**), by doing one job on which you are taxed properly while keeping quiet about other income (**moonlighting**), or by not passing everything through the till. More crudely it can involve claiming expenses you never incurred, or even claiming that you are entitled to a married couple's allowance when you aren't married. All forms of evasion are illegal and there are stiff penalties awaiting those caught at it. See Chapter 12.

Avoidance means <u>legally</u> reducing your tax bills. This involves claiming any deductions, or altering the way you do something to reduce or postpone the tax payable. This is your right to cut your tax bills within the limits of the law, and there are no penalties for cutting your tax in this way. On the contrary, you get money that, often, you are intended to get. For instance, anyone who wants to buy a personal pension gets full tax relief on the premium. You need not, as a self-employed person, do this, but if you do the government, in effect, will pay part of the cost. Some kinds of avoidance aren't there deliberately, but because of history, or a mistake. Why it's there does not matter to you - either way, if you take the right steps, you pay less.

There should be two stages to your handling of tax matters. The first is tax **planning**. This is where the cutting starts. You should allow for tax when planning what to do. Look at things **post-tax**, that is, after tax has been paid and allowances granted. In my book *Running Your Own Business* I urge readers to `Plan the 5 Ps' -

AVOIDANCE AND
EVASION - THE
DIFFERENCE

DO PLAN AND
DO COMPLY

purpose, products, potential, people, pounds. In each case, there is some aspect of your planning that may be affected by tax - sometimes quite sharply. I repeat here what I say there - plan it!

The tail should not wag the dog. Do not be one of those who devise everything just so as not to pay tax. There is no point investing in some useless machine just because the cost is tax-deductible. Do not set up some complicated arrangement that totally changes the way the business runs just to save a little tax. It may suit some people to keep permanently on the move so that they are never caught by any tax authority, but it rarely works - unless they never buy or sell anything either.

REMEMBER!
THE TOP TOP RATE IS NOW ONLY 40%!

When the top rate of income tax was 98% (and it is less than 20 years ago since that was so!) ... and the top rate of death duties was 80% (and that's quite recently, too) ... and the top rate of tax on gifts could be a startling 300% (as it was not so long ago) ... and the top rate of tax on gains from land was going to be a straight 100% (yep - the lot!)... people went to great lengths to avoid these rates.

Things are now radically different. **There is now no single rate of tax over 40% for any of the main taxes**, whether income tax, capital gains tax, corporation tax, NI, VAT or death duties.

At the same time, it is harder to avoid tax than it was when the rates were much higher. The most artificial of the dodges people used when tax rates were much higher have now been stopped - either by the courts or in Parliament - by **anti-avoidance** measures. These are rules designed expressly to stop people avoiding tax, for example by allowing the tax authorities to ignore transactions which you have entered into just to save tax. These rules stop you not paying, and mean your plans to sidestep have been a waste of time and money. Their effects must be watched, but they are limited in most cases to stopping `clever' avoidance tricks, where people do things not for a proper commercial reason, but only - or mainly - to reduce tax. If you think you have spotted a clever wheeze to avoid tax, you may be right. (Like other people, you probably won't shout about it if you find it works). However, if what you are doing is purely to avoid tax, don't be surprised if the tax officials have got there first.

The other stage besides planning is what the professionals call tax **compliance.** This is making sure you have met your legal obligations by registering with the tax authorities, making **returns** to them, and paying tax bills. Your business needs to meet the separate requirements of each tax, because the rules for each tax are different, as are the officials handling them. People often get help with their tax bills, and our next chapter looks at this.

AVOIDING AVOIDANCE

2   *Who's who in tax?*

*T*HIS CHAPTER is about the two sides to the game of tax - at least that is how many would have you view it. If your affairs are straightforward, there may be no "game". If you have checked your entitlement, you may not need a team; just do it yourself. However, a good tax adviser may earn his or her fee several times over. You will find plenty of experts prepared to help you with your tax - at a price. Is it a price worth paying?

PROFESSIONAL ADVICE

Many small businesses employ an accountant to "do the books". Most then get their accountants to do their tax affairs as well. That can be both good and bad. Most help with both tax compliance and tax planning. They often earn their fees back, and more, with the tax they save as a result.

At the other end there are, sadly, a number of incompetent advisers about. You need to be wary of them. They trade on your (and often their own) ignorance. Because of the requirements of secrecy on government officials, incompetent advisers can have quite an easy life. You don't know, do you, whether the income tax they say you have to pay is more or less than it should be? What is more, if the accountant gets things wrong, he can often put the blame on the tax authorities. It is said to be their fault that you are suddenly faced with paying a large tax bill. Is it? Rather too many taxpayers are ready to assume it is, even though they don't know.

Of course, tax officials make mistakes, but I know from experience that some tax advisers make them too, without their clients realising it. This is not surprising. Anyone can set up in business as a "tax accountant" or "tax adviser" without passing a single examination in anything, or knowing anything at all about our tax system. Most tax inspectors have blacklists of local firms they don't like, but you won't find out who's on it. You should check the firm you choose consists of professionally qualified people and has a good reputation.

YOU'S WHO

What you must remember is that you are responsible for the errors of your advisers. You may be able to sue your advisers for negligence if they get it wrong. This will not impress the tax authorities. They still want tax and penalties from you. If you make a wrong return for VAT - for example, you put the wrong figures in the standard return - you are at fault. This is so even if you employed someone else to do it for you. You will be told that you should have employed someone who did not make mistakes - and you should have checked what they were doing. The signature on the form will always be yours. So are the mistakes. So are the penalties.

DO I HAVE TO APPOINT
A TAX EXPERT?

No. The Revenue may prefer it (provided the person you appoint is not on the black list) because it may make life easier for them. The VAT staff will come to visit you whether or not you employ someone else. The only thing they can ask you for is information. In a small business, you may be able to handle this yourself. Some people are happy to get an accountant to help them in the first years to set up a pattern that they can then follow themselves.

It has been the practice of all companies to employ accountants to make the statutory returns. The government has announced that this rule will be changed for small companies. It will be even more important then to consider what help is needed in keeping the tax records right. It may be that a good bookkeeper (full- or part-time) is better than an expensive outsider. It may be that a good standard computer program is what you really need.

WHO CAN HELP?

Before appointing an expert, identify your problems. For example, if you are in business on your own part time, earning under £15,000, you do not have a problem. You do not pay VAT. Your social security position is simple. The Inspector of Taxes will only need a three-line account from you (income, expenses, and profit). You do not need outside help with that if you keep proper records. In many other small businesses, the problem may be VAT rather than income tax. Sort out your books to deal with that, and get the expert help there if you need it. Then think about the income tax. For example, if you make a loss, you pay no income tax - but you still have to pay VAT.

Tax officials are, in most offices, more helpful than they used to be. There are, unfortunately, some inconsiderate tax officials - but there are inconsiderate taxpayers too. Later in this chapter we consider who your tax officials are. Do not assume they will not help you. They have instructions to help : you are now the customer. They also have several series of useful detailed guides. It is worth checking with them.

If you are bringing in an expert, make sure he or she is just that. Do not employ anyone to handle your tax affairs unless you check their professional qualifications or their local reputation, or both. The advantage of employing a member of a regulated profession is perhaps greater for tax matters than for others. This is because tax laws change fast. It is easy to become an out-of-date tax expert, but it is of little use to the client. You need to know that someone on whom you are relying is checking the changes.

However, there is no <u>one</u> tax profession. Tax professionals can be involved in three separate professions: accountants, lawyers, and tax practitioners. There are also some former tax officials who practise as independent advisers. To complicate things, you should not assume that all accountants or all lawyers are tax specialists. They are not.

ACCOUNTANTS

The senior body of accountants is the Institute of **Chartered Accountants**. There are separate Institutes for England and Wales, Scotland and Ireland. Recently the English institute also set up a separate **Tax Faculty**. A chartered accountant (CA) has to have passed tough examinations before being allowed to qualify. He or she will also have served a training contract with other chartered accountants. In sitting for the examinations, they will have had to learn some tax, but they may have had no other training in it. The Tax Faculty was established to allow tax specialists to work together in association with the Institute. Faculty members must be tax experts, but do not have to be chartered accountants.

There are also other bodies of accountants, notably the **Certified Accountants**. They must also have passed examinations and undergone training, including some work in tax, to qualify. Both bodies also require their members to undertake regular continuing education to keep themselves up to date, but this need not include tax.

HELP FROM SOLICITORS

All solicitors receive some training in tax affairs. Commercial firms of solicitors are often geared up to give particularly useful advice in dealing with company taxation and corporate finance. Others are experts only in personal matters, such as inheritance tax. As with accountants, not all solicitors deal, or should deal, with tax matters, so - again - check up on whether a firm deals with much tax work, and on its local reputation. The Law Society (the solicitors' professional organisation, which also exerts disciplinary control over all practising solicitors) is currently working on introducing a tax diploma to show basic tax competence, although specialists are still best identified by reputation.

THE INSTITUTE OF
TAXATION

There is one specialist body just for tax, the **Chartered Institute of Taxation**. It has set up a junior branch, the **Association of Tax Technicians.** The members of both the Institute and the Association are tax practitioners who have passed specialist examinations in tax. Those who have completed the basic examinations and training can use the abbreviation ATT or description "tax technician". Tax practitioners - fellows or associates of the Institute - may also be qualified accountants or solicitors, but some are tax advisers with this qualification alone. They use the initials **FTII** or **ATII**. Tax practitioners have passed tough specialist examinations and agreed to the Institute's codes of conduct. They also have to keep themselves up to date, but can only do so by reference to taxation.

Banks and other financial businesses will also help. You can get advice about any kind of tax-saving proposals, such as leasing schemes or savings, from those who supply the schemes and products. They are also bound by working codes that should ensure that they give you the best advice for your circumstances. If thinking about any of these aspects, shop around. The national newspapers - in their Saturday editions - do a great job in helping keep people up to date on these schemes. There is also help available from the tax offices themselves, both as leaflets and guides, and as individual advice on particular queries. I know more than one person who went along to the local tax office to get help with some tax problem, and came away with some useful tips on tax-saving they hadn't expected!

OTHER SOURCES
OF HELP

That's what the envelope says that will bring your VAT and income tax demands. Of course,

ON HER MAJESTY'S
SERVICE

Her Majesty is not to blame. Don't forget our tax laws are put in place by politicians. If you don't like them, don't blame the Inland Revenue, Customs and Excise, or the DSS either. It's not their fault that the tax is due. It's the fault of MPs and Her Majesty's Ministers. It is this - and previous - governments who are responsible for laying down the rules that tax officials have to put into effect. In this book we try to avoid taking sides. It is not for us to reason why. That does not mean that you should not make your mind up about what is the good news and what is the bad news.

CUSTOMS

Her Majesty's Customs and Excise, as it is proud to call itself, is the oldest English government department. However, it is not really a customs department any longer. That is now all European work. Its main tax job now is running the VAT. If you register for VAT, a VAT officer will come and visit you for a control visit. The officer will be from your local VAT office. These are based in all large towns. The headquarters is in Southend. All local offices are linked to it by a computer network, and you are asked to deal with Customs (as it is known) through your local office even if this results in officials elsewhere dealing with your case.

Customs also deals with the excise taxes and, on behalf of the European Union, with customs duties. The department provides the Waterguard Service that patrols our frontiers to deal with drugs and contraband. This is, however, entirely separate from the VAT work.

THE REVENUE

Income tax is dealt with by an entirely different government department to VAT. The official title is the **Inland Revenue** (often abbreviated to IRC or Revenue). It is run, like Customs, by Commissioners, the senior civil servants in charge of the Inland Revenue Department. It is the job of the Inland Revenue to handle income tax, CGT, corporation tax, inheritance tax, stamp duties and the valuation of land for business rates. They also help the DSS collect most NI contributions.

Revenue staff are divided into several sections, run by a central organisation the head office of which is at Somerset House, on the Strand in London. You will need to be in touch with your local **Inspector of Taxes**. Inspectors are responsible for settling how much income tax, CGT or corporation tax is payable. Inspectors are based in local offices throughout the country, each in charge of a tax **district**. The local office bears the name of its district - anything from my own former tax district (ominously named `Tower') to London Provincial offices (which are everywhere but London). As those two examples show, your local tax district is not necessarily very `local', but that is where your papers will be handled.

Separate from the inspectors are the **Collectors of Tax**. These officers (though increasingly these days they seem to be computers!) have the job of checking you pay what is due from you.

Questions about the value of land are dealt with locally by another set of local offices, **District Valuers Offices**. They are responsible not only for land values for capital gains tax and similar purposes, but also for setting rateable values for local rates. Inheritance tax is handled by the **Capital Taxes Office**, and stamp duties by regional **Stamp Duty Offices**, again separate parts of what you can see is a big organisation.

THE SOCIAL

Next is the **DSS,** the Department of Social Security. In the last few years this has been divided into several executive agencies. The one responsible for NI contributions is the **Contributions Agency**, based in the north east of England. There is also a separate **Benefits Agency** that deals with entitlement to, and payment of, social security benefits. Both the Contributions Agency and the Benefits Agency have local inspectors, based in the local Social Security Office. These offices are also now linked by computers to headquarters, and, as with VAT, you should contact the Agency through the officials at your local office.

THE TOWN HALL

You will get your business rates bill and council tax bill from the Treasurer's Department of your local council. In practice, there is little to argue about in settling how much you pay. The main source of dispute is the value of property. That is determined by the Revenue's District Valuation Offices.

GETTING IN TOUCH

You must provide information to officials of each of these groups at certain times. When and how you do it is set out in the appropriate parts of this book. You will find that the local officials can offer you advice about the taxes in their care. All three government departments produce a series of detailed and useful summaries about the taxes they handle, and about particular problems. These are in the form of booklets and leaflets and they are free from local offices - you only need to ask. Again, we give details as we go along.

You will usually find officers will help with

advice as well, and help with claims. They clearly cannot run your tax affairs for you, but they may give you some practical help with points you hadn't thought about. Experience and training have both taught them to view the taxpayer as the `other side', and most taxpayers treat them in the same way - more so than in some neighbouring countries. So it is worth summarising some of the ground rules on which tax officials have to operate.

Notify the tax authorities in the right way when your business starts, and when you start employing someone.

WHAT TO DO WHEN STARTING

On the next page is a checklist of whom you must tell and when:

CHECKLIST: NOTIFYING THE TAX AUTHORITIES

1. The VAT Office for your area (find the address from your Phone Book under 'Customs and Excise'). You must notify them as soon as you are liable to register for VAT (see Chapter 4). This you do on Form VAT 1. There is a copy of this at the back of the book.

2. Your local Social Security Office (find out where by looking in the Phone Book under 'Social Security, Dept of' or 'Contributions Agency'). You must notify them if you are employing anyone, so that you can collect NI contributions owed by them (and you). Notify the Contributions Agency (which is usually at the local social security office) so that they can sort out your own liability to contributions, even if your earnings are low enough for you not to have to pay. Use Form CF 11 if you are becoming self-employed and will pay contributions, but Form CF 10 if you think you are entitled not to pay weekly contributions. There is another form, Form CF 351, available in leaflet NI 255 from Social Security Offices or Post Offices which allows you to pay contributions by direct debit.

3. The Inspector of Taxes for your district (find out your local district from the Phone Book under 'Inland Revenue'). The Inspector must be notified when you take on a member of staff who will earn more than about £55 a week, so that you can operate the PAYE system on the employee's pay. The Inspector must also be told when you start your business, so that returns can be sent to sort out any income tax due. You can give this notification on Form 41G.

If the business is run by a company, a slightly different form, CT 41G, is needed. If you were previously working for someone else, you should also send your P45 (given you by your last employer) to the Inspector.

One way of avoiding UK taxes is to leave the UK. That sounds obvious and simple. If you are a British citizen, you are also a citizen of the European Union, and you are probably based in the European Economic Area. From 1994 this involves Austria, Belgium, Denmark, Finland, France, Germany, Greece, Iceland, Ireland, Italy, Luxembourg, the Netherlands, Norway, Portugal, Spain, Sweden, and the United Kingdom in one vast customs union with freedom of movement within all these countries. However, anything happening outside the UK is likely to involve foreign tax. Not always - because there are **tax havens** where there is no or little tax. For example, the Cayman Islands do not have a tax system (instead, I am told, you may get eaten alive by the mosquitoes - you can't have everything!). Throughout the European Economic Area (EEA) taxes are at similar levels and are of similar kinds to ours. If you have connections with another state, or you start to do business outside the UK, you will probably end with a **double taxation** problem. This means that you will be paying tax in two places on the same transactions or profits. There will also be problems with VAT. If you are thinking of expanding overseas, or you have strong foreign connections, it is important that you get expert advice at the beginning from someone who knows the overseas position. In this book, for the sake of simplicity, we assume we are talking about United Kingdom tax and taxpayers only.

THE GLOBE-TROTTING
TAXPAYER

3   *Taxing your profits*

HOW INCOME TAX
WORKS

Y OU MUST pay the right amount of both income tax and NICs on your trading or professional profits. If you have income of any other kind (see the list in Chapter 1), you will pay income tax but not NICs on it. In practice, the Revenue may let you put small amounts of other income (eg rent for subletting a room in the office) into the business accounts. Where you have two distinct sources of income - as where someone is both self-employed and an employee - they must be kept separate. This is because different rules apply to each kind of income. In this chapter we look at how income tax works, and at the rules for taxing trading income. Rules applying only to companies are dealt with in Chapter 7.

Income tax is an annual tax. It is a tax on the total income of all kinds you receive each year. The rules require that each year all the taxable kinds of income you receive are totalled up. You are allowed some deductions from that total, such as a **personal allowance** and **interest relief.**

The balance left is your **taxable income** for the year, on which you pay income tax at that year's rates.

Tax rates are reviewed every year. Like governments in many states, our present government is committed to reducing income tax rates. Current rates are set out in the box, along with the main allowances.

THE INCOME TAX RATES AND ALLOWANCES FOR 1994-95

Lower rate of income tax 20%
[This is paid on the first £3,000 of taxable income,and on dividends]

Basic rate of income tax 25%

Higher rate of income tax..............................40%
[This is payable on each £1 of income, once the taxable income of the taxpayer exceeds £23,700]

Single personal allowance...........................£3,445

Married couple's allowance........................£1,720
[A single parent may also get this allowance]
Higher amounts are payable to those over retirement age and the blind

THE INCOME TAX YEAR

In the box on income tax rates we mention **1994-95**. This refers to the **income tax year** starting in 1994. This starts on 6 **April** each year (Why? Because it did last year...and that's what they said last year too). The government's financial year (and the tax year for companies and for most taxes) starts appropriately on All Fools' Day, 1 **April**. Because the income tax year straddles two calendar years - it runs through to 5 April the following year - the abbreviation 1994-95 refers to an income tax year. For companies, the reference is different. The **Financial Year 1994** means the Corporation Tax year starting on 1 April 1994, and running to 31 March 1995.

HOW MUCH INCOME
TAX DO I PAY?

The total income tax payable depends on your total income and allowances for the income tax year. For example, suppose you earn in total £25,000 in 1994-95, and you are single. You are entitled to a personal allowance of £3,445. You can earn this much before paying any tax. So you have £21,555 (£25,000 less £3,445) taxable pay. £3,000 of this is taxed at 20%, a total of £600 tax. The next £18,555 is taxed at 25%, a total of £4,638. Your tax bill will be £5,238, if you have no other deductions. It's worth noting that the average rate of tax paid in this example is about 21 per cent (the total tax divided by the total income).

Every individual is entitled to a personal allowance, regardless of age. Those over retirement age are entitled to higher allowances, with more again at 80.

Since 1990, it matters little for income tax whether you are married or living with someone else. Before that, the income of married couples was added together, but husband and wife are both now taxed separately. The couple can claim a **married couple's allowance**, although since 1994 this is of diminishing value. The amount of the allowance is £1,720. For 1993-94 relief was available on that sum at the basic rate. In 1994-95, relief is limited to the lower rate of 20 per cent. In 1995-96, relief is restricted to 15 per cent of the sum only, worth £258. It is likely to be abolished in due course. It cannot be claimed by unmarried couples, although a single parent bringing up a child on her or his own can claim it.

Both husband and wife receive their own personal allowance. If the wife (or husband) is not working, it cannot be transferred to the other partner, and is lost. One way of cutting the couple's tax bills is to ensure that the working partner employs the other partner to help in the business. This is common practice. She or he usually earns a sum less than both the personal allowance and the lower level of payment for NI contributions on employees. In 1994-95, that is about £2950. See Chapter 9.

Income tax is based on the total of all kinds of income taxable in that year. This does not mean that the income is either earned or received in that year. For most kinds of income (such as interest, dividends and earnings) that is true, but the rules for trading income are complicated. They are also changing between 1994 and 1997. This is because the Revenue is introducing **Self-Assessment.**

TRADING ACCOUNTS
YEARS AND TAX YEARS

From 1996-97 all individual taxpayers must make a self-assessment of their income tax and capital gains tax liability for that and subsequent years. They will have an option, provided they meet earlier deadlines, to have their income assessed as now. This change follows the introduction of **pay and file** for companies, described in Chapter 7. It also follows a practice currently adopted by some trading taxpayers for their own convenience.

Another major change for all traders comes in from 1996-97. For that year and subsequent years tax on trading income will be payable on the profits for that year. This rule applies to those starting new trades from 1994-95. Why is this important?

Until 1994-95, income tax on trades was always charged on a **preceding year basis**. The profits taxed in any one year were based on the profits made by the business in the accounts year that ended in the preceding tax year. For example, if you run your accounts on a calendar year basis, the accounts end on 31 December. The accounts on which your tax bill is based in 1992-93 are therefore not the accounts for 1992 and 1993, but the accounts year that ended in 1991-92. This is the set of accounts for the trading year ending 31 December 1991.

This rule allowed taxpayers to cut their tax bills by careful timing and arrangement. For example, if you run your accounts on a tax year basis, then you pay tax on your income for the year ending 5 April 1992 in the tax year 1992-93, about 12 months later. If you run your accounts on an accounts year running from 1 May to 30 April you pay tax on your income for the year ending 30 April 1992 in the tax year 1993-94, a whole year later. You would not have to pay tax on profits earned at the beginning of that accounts year (May 1992) until you paid your tax bills for 1993-94 (in 1995).

THE NEW RULES

If a business is started on or after 6 April 1994, then the new rules will apply to it. Under these rules, tax will be payable in any tax year on the profits of that year, or of the accounts period which ends in that year. For example, you start a new business on 1 January 1995. The accounts run for calendar years. In 1995-96, tax will be due on the accounts for the calendar year 1995. If your business had started on 1 January 1990, you would be paying tax in 1995-96 on the accounts for the calendar year 1994.

For businesses started before that date, the old rules continue to apply until 1996-97 (that is, for both 1994-95 and 1995-96). Transitional rules will phase businesses over from the old system to the new system, but these are not due until the Finance Bill 1995.

The rules for self-assessment were introduced in 1994. From 1996, you must make returns on your business by 31 January following the end of the tax year (31 January 1997 for 1995-96). You have to work out the total tax due to the Revenue from your income and gains for the year. Any outstanding tax will be due on that date. Late returns will be subject to automatic penalties. However, if you do not want to work out your tax, you have the choice of making an earlier return of information only. If you return all the necessary information to the Revenue by 30 September of the year in which the tax year ends, the Revenue will work out the tax liability for you. For example, for 1995-96, you will have to have your return with the Revenue by 30

September 1996 to take advantage of this. Any unpaid tax will be due, as before, on 31 January next.

ACCOUNTS IN THE FIRST FEW YEARS

Neither the old (preceding year) rules, nor the new rules, work tidily during the first year of a new business. This appears from the example of the business starting on 1 January 1995. Under both sets of rules, the business is taxed on its actual profits for the first tax year. In the example this is from 1 January 1995 to 5 April 1995, although this will usually be assumed to be one quarter of its first year profits.

Under the old rules, in the second year, tax is paid on the profits of the first twelve months of the business. In the third year, tax is paid on the preceding year basis (ie the accounts year ending in the second year.) This is the first twelve months again! Under the new rules, this problem does not arise. The business is usually taxed on the right basis in the second year, avoiding overlap.

The effect of the old rules was to tax people twice or even three times on their opening profits. There was therefore a strong temptation to avoid making profits in the first year. Above all, it was unwise to have large profits in that year followed by lower profits in later years. The new rules avoid much distortion, but the overlap still occurs and there still is scope for cutting tax bills by choosing the right opening date for a business.

Income tax trading rules take account of the accounts year of the business. How far are they based on the accounts themselves? That is the subject of the rest of this chapter, and the next two chapters. We shall see that the answer is: partly. To give some idea of the problems, a simple set of profit and loss accounts are set out on the next pages to suggest points to be watched.

ACCOUNTS AND TAX

How Accounts Should be Adjusted for Tax Reasons

Favoured Floggles

Profit and Loss Account for the Year Ending 31 March 199...'

	£	£
Turnover		120,000
Cost of sales:		
Opening stock	4,000	
Purchases	64,000	
	68,000	
Less closing stock	8,000	
Gross Profit		(60,000)
		60,000
add rental income		2,000
		62,000
Expenses		
Staff pay	30,000	
Own and staff NI	4,000	
Rent and rates	5,000	
Heat and light	600	
Telephone	1,000	
Repairs and improvements	2,400	

Annotations:

If you make the adjustments necessary and desirable to these accounts, what is FF's taxable profit? You will find it is rather different from the loss claimed!

Why end the year then? Why not 30 April?

Assuming most supplies are standard-rated, Fab should be registered for VAT. If so, all VAT should be left out of these accounts

Opening and closing stock must be valued on the same basis

Rental income should be dealt with separately

Class 1 and half Class 4 contributions are deductible, but not Class 2

Does this include personal calls? They are not allowable

Repairs can be deducted, but not improvements

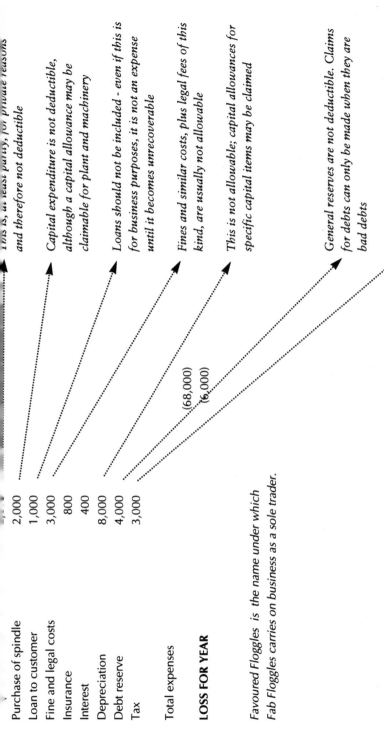

...is, at least partly, for private reasons and therefore not deductible

Capital expenditure is not deductible, although a capital allowance may be claimable for plant and machinery

Loans should not be included - even if this is for business purposes, it is not an expense until it becomes unrecoverable

Fines and similar costs, plus legal fees of this kind, are usually not allowable

This is not allowable; capital allowances for specific capital items may be claimed

General reserves are not deductible. Claims for debts can only be made when they are bad debts

Income tax (and CGT - or Corporation tax) cannot be deducted as an expense - it is one way you spend your profits!

Purchase of spindle	2,000
Loan to customer	1,000
Fine and legal costs	3,000
Insurance	800
Interest	400
Depreciation	8,000
Debt reserve	4,000
Tax	3,000
Total expenses	(68,000)
LOSS FOR YEAR	(6,000)

Favoured Floggles is the name under which Fab Floggles carries on business as a sole trader.

As the model accounts suggest, the basic rule is that ordinary commercial accounts cannot be used without adjustment as tax accounts. This is so even though an auditor has certified the accounts as `true and fair' under the Companies Acts.

TRADING PROFITS: THE
BASIC RULES

In calculating the profits of a business in any year for income tax purposes, what are needed are the following figures, which are taken, after adjustment, from the trading accounts :

The total income from the business for the year (excluding any capital sums received)

The total allowable expenditure of the year in running the business

The opening stocks of materials or inventory at the start of the year

The closing stocks at the end, valued in the same way as the opening stocks

Capital allowances and other adjustments will be made to the taxable profits to work out tax payable.

Taxable Profits, The Basic Formula:

TAXABLE PROFITS FOR THE YEAR =

	INCOME
+	**CLOSING STOCK**
−	**OPENING STOCK**
−	**EXPENSES**

Should the accounts show what the business has earned, or what cash it has received during the year? There may be a considerable difference between these figures. The Revenue usually insists, after the opening years of the business, that accounts are on an **earnings basis.** The accounts must show what has been earned even if it has not been paid for. This means that, for example, an item is treated as sold, or a service as completed, when the goods are delivered and the bill is sent out rather than when it is paid. The rule is similar to the main rule for VAT (though smaller businesses may swap to cash accounting for VAT in many cases).

The Revenue usually insist that most businesses, (unless very small) are run on an earnings basis after the opening period. The alternative is a **cash basis**. This is available to most smaller businesses for VAT purposes on request. In this method the accounts record all payments in and out when they are made rather than when they are earned. For instance, say that you send a bill to a customer, and the customer takes two months to pay. On the earnings basis, the amount the customer owed you should go into the accounts when the bill is sent. On a cash basis, it goes into the accounts only when the customer actually pays.

CASH OR EARNINGS?

The problem with the earnings rule is that - inevitably - not everyone pays up. You become liable to pay tax when you send out the bill, but you may never be paid if the debtor becomes insolvent. Most wiser businessmen allow for that and have a bad debts reserve. Maybe, but the tax authorities won't wear that. You can deduct unpaid debts only when they become bad debts, that is, they are not reasonably collectable.

BAD DEBTS

YOUR OWN DEBTS

The same rule works in reverse on the bills incurred by the business. These should go into the accounts when the bills are incurred, rather than when the business pays them. Again, the speed of incurring debts can be accelerated or decelerated near the end of the accounts year if there seems good reason to do so.

TRADING INCOME

Two issues need to be sorted out in deciding whether a sum is to be included as income in the profit and loss accounts of a business. First, is the sum income from that trade or profession or is it received for some other reason? That raises two questions - when is something *"from"* the business, and what is a **"trade"** or **"profession"**? Sums received from other sources, such as rent, are taxed under other rules. Exceptionally, the sum may not be taxable at all but may, for example, be a gift to the trader (as there is no tax on genuine personal gifts). This is unusual. It arises only where a trader has no contractual right to, or expectation of, a payment that is made either by a customer who has ceased trading with the trader or by someone who is not a customer. They might take the form of a prize, such as a literary prize given to someone for something out of the ordinary. They may be gifts left by someone in a will, for example, to a hairdresser or doctor.

WHAT ARE TRADES AND PROFESSIONS?

The precise words in law are "trade", "profession" and "vocation", but it matters little whether something is described as one or the other. Two points only need watching:

Self-supply - if you use your own trading stock, you must treat the supply as a sale, and put it in the accounts. If you supply yourself with services, eg doctors diagnosing themselves or a carpenter repairing the family furniture, you do not have to account for the time spent. Otherwise, lawyers' bills might be even larger!

One-offs - you may be trading although you only buy and sell something once. You don't become a journalist by writing one article for the newspapers. One-off items are taxable, but under different rules that have the effect of charging the sums separately for the year in which they are received. The rules are in Schedule D Case VI in the tax laws.

There is no tidy definition of a **trade**. It includes any kind of activity manufacturing, importing or creating goods, or selling, hiring, lending, or providing services of any kind (except those that are professional). The fact that the trade is illegal or unique is irrelevant. It matters only that it is the sort of thing people do for a profit.

Professions are those activities that rely on personal intellectual skills. This is a rather snobbish tax rule. Lawyers are professionals and stockbrokers are not. Selling photographs might be a profession, but selling cameras is not.

The key common element to trades and professions is that they involve the direct earning of the profits with some offsetting revenue expenditure. They are separate from the activity of a landlord who earns money by letting his property at a rent. However, a landlord who also provides services, for example letting holiday homes where trips and facilities such as water-skiing are also provided, would also be a trader. Deciding whether something is income (which must go in the profit and loss account) or capital (which does not, but is taxable by CGT)is a more usual problem. It has caused many disputes between the Revenue and taxpayers in the past. The chief reason for the disputes was a contrast between high rates of income tax, and low rates of CGT. Indeed, there was no tax on capital profits until the 1960s. Since 1988, capital gains of both companies and individuals have been taxed at the same rates as income. Since then, the differences between the tax treatment of income and the tax treatment of capital have been limited, although they can still be important. They largely do not matter for VAT purposes.

There are important differences in the treatment of capital expenditure and revenue expenses (see Chapters 5 and 6). Another difference is that inflation is allowed for in working out a capital gain, through the indexation allowance (also explained in Chapter 6). This is not available in working out income tax profits. Another important difference is that NI contributions are payable on income but not on capital receipts. Although it is not often worth arguing too hard over the finer aspects of the divide, it is still important. Its other likely importance for tax purposes is in claiming relief if there is a loss. The rules allowing relief for income losses are much more generous than those for capital losses (see Chapter 6). What is the difference between income and capital?

INCOME OR CAPITAL?

The line is one between profits from a trading-style transaction, and the sale of an investment or of part of the permanent capital base of a business. It is the difference between the circulating capital of the business as against the fixed capital. In borderline cases, tax officials look at such things as:

The length of time the item has been held before sale

How many times items like that have been sold by the trader

The reason for the sale

The kind of items sold.

What expenditure is, and what is not, allowable against trading income is dealt with in Chapter 5. Allowances for capital expenses are dealt with in Chapter 6.

Finally, you must take account of the trading stock to calculate the trading profit or loss for a year. This means the stock of items held at the beginning and end of each year for sale by or use in the business. For a service industry that is providing services rather than goods, account also needs to be taken of **work in progress.** This is the value of outstanding work done and to be done under contracts for which bills have not yet been prepared.

It is important to take account of trading stock and work in progress in working out the true profit of a business. It will be rare for a business to finish the year with the same level of stocks as at the start. However, the business will use its profits to buy new stock, and equally can save money by running down its stocks. Unless stock figures are taken into account, the cash figures of profit may be too high or too low.

TRADING STOCK

The Revenue require that tax accounts contain valuations for stock and work in progress at the beginning and end of each year. How should this be valued? In many trades there are well-established ways of valuing stock, and the Revenue will accept use of these. Apart from such methods, the Revenue cannot insist on any one method of stock valuation. They can require that the method is a fair one and is used consistently, so that over time it reveals the full profits of the business. It is not acceptable to change methods during the year in the hope of losing some profit. That the Revenue will correct.

VALUING THE STOCK

One widely used method is to value the stock at the lower of cost of buying the stock, and current market value. On most stock this means that the stock is held at its purchase value; but where stock has deteriorated or gone out of fashion, it can be written down to what it is likely to fetch when sold. This is the guide widely accepted by the accountancy profession, and laid down in one of the Accounting Standards Board's approved Statements of Standard Accountancy Practice. Where a particular industry uses its own rules for stock valuation, these will usually be accepted by the Revenue too, provided that they apply consistently and do not "hide" profits.

CHECKLIST FOR TAX CUTTERS

Claim your full personal allowances.

It may be worth a husband employing his wife so she may claim her personal allowance, or to transfer income on which he is paying 40 per cent tax to her.

Start your business, or your accounting year on the right date. Don't pay your tax before you need to.

Don't make too much profit in the first few months - you'll pay tax twice on it.

Remember to watch for the 1996-97 changes for existing businesses.

Towards the end of each year it may be worth watching incomings and outgoings. Is it better to incur bills quickly or slowly, to chase debtors or let things wait a bit?

You can't use your ordinary trading accounts without adjustment for income tax purposes.

Debts cannot be left out of your accounts unless they are bad debts.

Genuine gifts are not trading income and should be left out of your accounts.

If you supply yourself with a service, leave it out of the accounts.

If you supply yourself with trading stock, it should go into the accounts.

Watch the difference between income and capital; the same rate of tax now applies but the allowances are different.

4   *Must I pay VAT?*

*A*LMOST THE entire world has now adopted value added tax (VAT) as the way to tax sales of goods and services. We adopted VAT in the United Kingdom when we joined the European Community. VAT is not only the main sales tax throughout the Community. It is imposed in every state in Europe, and is a major tax in every other part of the world. In other words, if you are in the business of supplying either goods or services, then you are likely to find yourself involved with VAT whether you like it or not. It isn't about to go away.

Although VAT is now one of the most important taxes in the UK a surprising number of people still try to ignore it. The general attitude seems to be that you just fill in the forms you are given and let it happen! Few businesses adopt the same attitude to income tax. The result is that people may pay too much tax. Equally, they may find themselves landed with large penalties for errors that they did not anticipate making. Either is expensive. VAT should be at the forefront of your thinking about taxation. That is why this chapter is at the front of this book.

The tax is proving so popular with governments partly because it raises huge sums of money at what seem fairly low rates of tax. It is also because the idea of VAT is simple and fair (even if the reality seems something other!).

VAT is potentially a tax on everything. Every time a supply of either goods or services is made, the supplier will be **adding value** to what is supplied (unless selling at below cost). If the supply is within the scope of VAT, then tax must be added at the set rate of the total sale price. This imposes VAT on the full value of the sale. At the same time, the seller can set off the amount of VAT paid by him in creating or obtaining the goods. The result is that he collects tax on the full value, but sets off the amount paid by him to others, for the value they added. The result is that the tax he collects reflects the value added by him. The box on the next page gives an example of this.

Looked at another way, VAT is a tax on the profit margin made by a supplier together with the overheads incurred by the supplier direct. In practice, the main overhead is the cost of staff. Another cost on which the seller collects VAT without paying it on to others is that of finance (for example, loan interest). For example, you buy goods for £1,000, and incur £200 staff costs and £20 finance costs in handling the goods. You make a profit of £500 in selling the goods for £2,000 after taking account of those and all other overheads. All the other overheads are paid for to others subject to VAT (for example, electricity). The value you add is £720. This is your profit, your staff costs and your finance costs. Your customer must pay VAT on those, and you must pay that VAT to Customs.

HOW VAT WORKS

Al runs a business producing hand-embroidered material. Unknown to Al, Beth buys Al's products to make "folk" costumes. Beth sells folk costumes to Cath, a clothing wholesaler. Don is one of Cath's retailer customers, and he buys a particular folk cardigan that Ed recently bought from Don's shop for £120. At each stage of this chain, the supplier is in business, and makes a **standard-rated** supply for VAT purposes. That is, the seller adds 17.5 per cent VAT to the selling price. At each stage, the VAT Office only collects the VAT on the value added at <u>that</u> stage. Here's how it happens.

Stage 1 :
Al sells material to Beth for £15 plus VAT (a price of £17.63). For simplicity's sake, assume Al paid nothing for the thread and other stuff used in the material. Al will collect the £2.63 VAT and pay it to the VAT Office.

Stage 2 :
Beth makes the cardigan, and sells it to Cath for £40 plus VAT (a total of £47). Beth collects £7 VAT, but can recoup the £2.63 VAT she paid Al from this. She pays the VAT Office the difference, £4.37.

Stage 3 :
Cath sells the cardigan to Don for £60 plus VAT, a total of £70.50. Cath collects £10.50 VAT, but spent £7 on the cardigan, which she recoups, sending £3.50 to the VAT Office.

Stage 4 :
Don sells the cardigan to Ed for £120. Don does not add VAT to his prices, so he has to pay the VAT Office out of the £120. For VAT purposes, he is treated as selling the cardigan to Ed for the sum that, when he adds VAT at 17.5 per cent, gives the total of £120. This works out at £102.13, plus VAT of £17.87. Don will pay the £17.87, less the £10.50 he paid, to the VAT Office.

HOW THE VAT WAS PAID

Ed paid a total of £17.87 VAT on the cardigan, and the VAT Office collected that much - but not from Ed. Instead they were paid:

£ 2.63	by Al
£ 4.37	by Beth
£ 3.50	by Cath
£ 7.37	by Don
£17.87	together on the full final sale price of the cardigan

Each has therefore paid the VAT Office tax on the amount of value added by her or him (that is the amount spent on improving or selling the product, plus the profit made in doing so)

VAT does not apply to everything sold or supplied. In particular it does not apply to a supply by a private person. The law provides that VAT may only be collected by a person who is a **taxable person**. To be a taxable person, an individual or company must be carrying on a business where the turnover of the total of all business dealings exceeds set limits. These limits (which are revised every year) are set out in the box overleaf.

WHEN YOU ARE LIABLE
FOR VAT

WHEN YOU HAVE TO REGISTER FOR VAT: THE 1994-95 FIGURES

You **must** register for VAT within one month of your turnover exceeding, or being predicted to exceed, the following limits:

Total turnover over the last 12 months of at least £45,000, or

Predicted turnover over the next month of at least £45,000

The 12 and one month periods are counted afresh every month.

These figures are revised every year. For figures for other years ask the VAT Office for their free leaflet *Should I Be Registered For VAT?*

The £45,000 limit (or figures for other years) represents total taxable **turnover**, not profits. Taxable turnover means sales or other supplies of goods or services liable to VAT. You are still liable to register for VAT if you have turnover at this level although you are making a loss.

Total turnover must include all the businesses you carry on. For instance, if your main business is running an antique shop, but you also regularly write articles for magazines, you must include both the shop profits and the article fees in your turnover. It does not include businesses run by others. For example, if you write the articles, but the antique shop is run by your wife, or by a partnership of you and your wife, the shop and your writing have to be looked at separately to see if both or either must register. However, the VAT Office has powers to stop fiddling by dividing a business between different people. If you deliberately split up a business, for example between two small companies, then the VAT Office can require you to register them as one taxpayer if the total turnover of all the businesses exceeds the limit.

If your business, or businesses, have total taxable turnover exceeding the annual limit, it is vitally important that you register for VAT as soon as possible. Failing to register does not protect you from paying the tax. You are still liable for the tax you should have collected as if you had been registered. You may also incur interest and stiff penalties. Further, you may lose the right to collect back any VAT you paid out during the period.

WHAT IF I DON'T HAVE TO REGISTER

If you are carrying on a business, you have the right to register voluntarily, even if you are not required to do so. If you are carrying on business at a lower level of turnover, or if you are intending to carry on a business, but are only just getting started, it may be an advantage to register voluntarily. This is for several reasons. First, you may not wish people to know that your turnover is less than the set figures. If you fail to register, they will assume your turnover is below the limit. That may be bad publicity. Another reason is that you have to be registered to claim back any VAT you pay out. If the business is going to have to be registered anyway later, it may pay to register while you are paying out the big bills on new equipment. Similarly, even if you do not expect the business to grow to achieving the turnover levels, it may be better to claim input tax back at the beginning.

The final reason for being registered is that it may make your prices lower. This may sound odd. How can your prices be cheaper when you put them up? The answer depends on who your customer is. If you are selling to someone who is VAT registered, they can claim back any VAT they pay you. If you are registered for VAT, you can, in effect, knock the VAT out of your prices. Take the example of Cath earlier in this chapter. She bought a cardigan for £40 plus £7 VAT, and sold it for £60 plus £10.50 VAT. If Cath is not registered for VAT, she pays £47, not £40 for the cardigan, because she cannot recover the tax. To make the same profit when selling on to Don, she must sell for £67. This may seem less than the £70.50 including VAT, but if Don is registered for tax, it actually costs him £7 more! This is because he can get the VAT back, but cannot reclaim the extra £7 VAT she has charged him indirectly. Consequently, buyers usually prefer VAT registered sellers. At the very least, it costs them nothing extra.

However, if your business will remain a small one with low turnover, you may find the hassle of VAT is not worth it. The government sets high levels so that really small businesses do not have to be involved with VAT if they do not want to be. These are most advantageous to small service businesses selling to private customers. There is an irony here. Unregistered traders often think they are getting away with tax by not being registered. In fact, they are often still paying most of the tax that would be due from them. This is because they are paying more for things such as heating, telephone bills, and items such as cars than they would if they collected VAT.

If you think you must register, contact your local VAT Office of Customs and Excise straight away. They will, if asked, let you have a VAT Pack, consisting of:

  The registration form (VAT 1)

  A booklet: *Should I Be Registered For VAT?*

  A booklet: *VAT Trade Classification*

  Other information leaflets

Customs have specialist leaflets on most businesses, with updated information. They will supply this to you on request from the local VAT Office.

You should register by using the form VAT 1. All that the VAT Office really need is your name, trading address, and a few basic details about the size and kind of business. The form must be returned to the VAT Office nearest your business address. For the address of a VAT Office, look in your local phone book under Customs and Excise.

When you have registered, you are known as a **registered person**, and you are subject to the requirements of the VAT laws until you cease to be registered. However, if you should have registered, but have not done so, you will still be treated as if you are a registered person.

Once registered, there are several standard procedures you must follow:

You must charge VAT on all **supplies** made by you which are standard-rated

You must keep full records of your business **inputs** and **outputs**

You must make regular returns to the VAT Office on the inputs and outputs of your business

With each return, you must send a cheque for the VAT collected by you, less the VAT paid out by you, during that period

You must give a proper **tax invoice** for the VAT charged if you make a taxable supply to another registered person.

If not registered, you must not add VAT to a bill. To do so is a criminal offence. Further, the VAT Office can collect the tax from someone if they catch them doing it, but will not allow any input tax deductions.

SUPPLIES

You **supply** goods or services any time you sell, exchange or give something to someone else as part of your business. For most purposes, whether the "something" is goods or services (or some of both together) does not matter. It is chiefly of concern when dealing with exports or imports, or when a VAT rate changes. You need to know then to work out precisely when a supply was made. Normally, these points don't cause problems. But you do have to check whether VAT does or does not attach to every sale or other supply. For example, it may apply to such things as giving goods or meals to employees or Christmas presents to business friends.

VAT is a tax of ins and outs, but just to confuse you the outs are called **inputs** and the ins are called **outputs**. Let me explain. Whenever a registered person makes a supply that is VATable, VAT must be added to the bill and collected by the supplier. This tax is known as **output tax**, although it is of course income. Whenever the supplier pays a bill for goods or services, he or she will pay VAT on that bill. This VAT is called **input tax**, although it is an outgoing. Whoever invented the phraseology for VAT clearly intended it to be different from income tax - but did they have to make up a whole new language?

All this talk of inputs and outputs is because it is the job of all registered businesses to account to the VAT Office for the difference between output tax and input tax, that is, between tax collected and tax paid. That difference will, as the example of the cardigan showed, amount to a tax on the value added to supplies by the supplier.

There are four ways in which supplies are treated for VAT purposes:

Supplies outside the scope of the tax. Supplies made by people who are not registered, or made outside the business context are not counted. Neither are most supplies of services or money that are not made for consideration, that is, for a price. If I make a gift of money to you, even in a business context, it is not a VATable supply by me to you, or by you to me.

Zero-rate supplies. Some kinds of supply are charged to VAT, but at a 0 per cent rate of tax. This means that the seller adds no VAT to the bill when making a supply. But the seller can claim a tax credit for any input tax paid out in making the supply (for example, on petrol or telephones). The important zero-rated items are listed below.

Exempt supplies. These are supplies on which the supplier cannot charge VAT, and cannot claim back any VAT incurred in making the supply. All the major exempted items are set out below.

Standard-rated supplies. Any supply that is neither zero-rated nor exempt is a standard-rated supply. If a supply is standard-rated, the supplier must add VAT at 17.5 per cent (the current standard rate) to the price when making the supply. This covers everything within the scope of VAT but not zero-rated or exempt supplies.

ZERO-RATED SUPPLIES:

The following goods and services are currently zero-rated:

Aircraft and air services, including selling and maintaining aircraft, passenger and freight transport by air, airport and other incidental charges

Animal food stuffs, but not pet foods

Books, magazines, newspapers, maps and leaflets

Caravans and houseboats designed to be lived in permanently

Charity supplies including supplies by them, eg through a charity shop, and some supplies to them - this also covers some supplies to the NHS

Children's clothing

Construction work on new homes and the sale of new homes and fixtures normally supplied in them, but not repairs or alterations, except to listed buildings, or architects, surveyors, and engineers fees,

Drinks (tea, coffee, etc) other than alcoholic drinks, fizzy drinks like lemonade, fruit juices, mineral waters

Exports of goods (goods are charged when they are imported to the country where they will be finally sold)

Food sold for human consumption (and not supplied to be eaten immediately), but the following are standard rated - chocolates, sweets and confectionery, ice cream and lollies and their ingredients, pet food, potato crisps and similar products, salted roasted nuts and other savoury snacks

Freight transport internationally

International services - the rules here are complicated. If supplying services outside the UK, check the position carefully.

Medicines supplied on prescription, and many kinds of supply made to blind or other disabled people

New homes sold, or leased for over 21 years, by the builders

Passenger transport by rail, coach, bus and other vehicles carrying 12 or more passengers, but not taxis or cars

Protective boots and helmets, but only if bought by individuals.

Ships and shipping services, including selling and servicing ships, passenger and freight transport and port charges

Take-away food supplied cold (eg sandwiches)

Tax-free shops - sales made to travellers in "duty free" shops are zero-rated

Water rates and charges, including sewerage charges, to private individuals

Note : For the year from April 1994, fuel supplies to domestic users are charged VAT at a reduced rate of 8 per cent. The full rate applies after that. Previously such supplies were zero-rated.

EXEMPT SUPPLIES:

The following supplies are currently exempted:

Bank and building society current, deposit and savings accounts (see also **Credit**)

Betting and gaming

Credit facilities including making advances and loans, hire purchase agreements and issuing debentures and similar securities

Education and training by schools or universities, or similar services not made for profit

Funerals, burials and cremations

Health services provided by doctors, dentists, opticians, nurses, pharmacists and the supplementary medical professions

Insurance and the work of agents and brokers related to insurance claims

Heritage property such as works of art given special tax status for inheritance tax and CGT

Land and building sales and the sale or letting of any right to use land or buildings, but not: camping, fishing, shooting, parking, storing boats or aircraft, holding sports events or exhibitions, holiday accommodation, hotel, guest house or similar services

Lotteries

Postal services supplied by the Post Office

Professional, pressure group and trade associations supplies to members

Sports competitions entry rights (but not charges for entering or using premises)

Tenancy agreements, except holiday lettings or hotel or similar residential accommodation

Trade union supplies to members

Welfare services and goods supplied by charities and public bodies, but not for profit

HOW TO CHARGE VAT

If you are making a standard-rate supply, you must add VAT at 17.5 per cent to the bill. Alternatively, you can choose not to add VAT to the bill, but you must then treat part of the price paid as the VAT (as Don did in the example about the cardigan). What you cannot do legally is to quote a price without mentioning VAT in any way, and then add it afterwards. If you intend to claim that the price is VAT-exclusive so VAT has to be added, you must do so before the sale unless it is clearly understood (for example because of previous dealings with that customer) that prices are VAT-exclusive. You can advertise or quote VAT-exclusive prices, as long as you put up a notice, or print a clause in your terms, saying so. Otherwise, you may be committing a criminal offence under the Trades Descriptions Act or other consumer protection legislation.

First, some more jargon. Ever had a **tax point**? No, it's not a thing to argue about. It's the technical term for the time at which VAT must be charged on a supply. There are complicated rules about this, but in summary, the position is:

Goods - the tax point is the earliest of: the date when the goods are removed from the supplier's premises, the date when the goods are paid for, or the date when a **tax invoice** is sent out by the supplier. In practice, if a tax invoice is issued within 14 days after the goods are physically supplied to the customer (or the customer pays, if earlier), then the date of issue of the invoice is the tax point.

Services - the tax point is the date when you have finished performing the services being supplied (except, of course, for sending out the bill!). Again, if the invoice is sent out within 14 days of that day, the date of the invoice is taken.

Of the amount included in the tax invoice, normally. If you make a supply, you must account for VAT even if you choose not to send out an invoice (for example, where you have supplied goods free to an employee as a present). In tricky cases such as this - or where you are selling cheap for non-commercial reasons - you should charge the VAT on the market value of the supply.

Discounts cause problems. The rules say that if you offer a customer a discount, and the discounted price is paid, VAT is charged only on the discounted price. This is also true where you set a price for a supply, but then reduce it for prompt payment - even if the customer pays late and so does not get the discount. Discounts that are left open (eg, `if you find the goods sold cheaper elsewhere in town this week, we will refund the difference') are to be ignored.

Problems are frequently caused because a supply is made up of several things. For instance, a mail-order supply will cover the goods, packaging and postal charges, and possibly credit charges too. Where the additional supplies, such as packaging, are incidental, and there is no separate charge, the whole supply is treated as the supply of the main item only. But where there is a separate charge for postage or an unusual amount of packing the supply has to be treated as a **mixed supply**.

The amount paid for **mixed** supplies, that is, supplies of two or more separate goods or services together, has to be divided. You must apply the VAT separately to each part of the supply. Even if a supply does not have to be divided, you can sometimes separate the parts yourself to reduce the overall VAT level. For example, if you supply goods under a credit sale to a customer who is paying a finance charge, you are making two supplies: the goods, probably standard-rated, and the credit, which is exempt. If you charge the two together without separating the finance charge, you must charge VAT on the lot.

TAX INVOICES

A **tax invoice** is the document you must issue when making a supply of an item within the scope of VAT, that is, your customer is also a VAT-registered business. This means that all businesses will need to have forms of VAT invoice available. To comply with the law, the invoice must set out required information to allow the customer to claim the tax. The VAT authorities will also use it to check on the transaction at both ends.

A simple form of invoice can be used where the total amount (including the tax) is not over £100. For transactions over £100, a full VAT invoice must be given. The diagrams show what the two must contain.

Your invoices must include the following, which are labeled by number on the diagrams

1	Your name and address
2	Your VAT number
3	Taxpoint (time of supply)
4	Description identifying the goods/services supplied including...
5	Quantity and charge
6	Cash discounts (if any)
7	VAT rate
8	Total charge, including VAT
9	Customer's name and address
10	Identification number

For suplues of less than £50 you can use a simple form of Invoice

---

WIBBLE WIDGETS [1]

32 Low St., Whiteburn, SN7 3QF

2

VAT No. 797 979797

3

Date....................199....

Desciption	Price
4	
Total	**10**
VAT rate 7	

For supplies of more than £50 you must use the full form of VAT invoice.

WIBBLE WIDGETS

32, Low Street
Whiteburn
SN7 3QF

Tel: 0798 4325675

VAT No. 797 979797
DATE ....199.... **3**

Customer's Name and Address

11

Account No.

Quantity	Product Code	Description	Discount	VAT Rate	Price	VAT
5		**6**	**7**			

				Totals	**8**	**9**
				Add VAT	**9**	
				Total Due		

Delivery Address and Instructions

SUPPLIED ON OUR
STANDARD TERMS AND
CONDITIONS

INVOICE NUMBER :   **12**

By now it will be clear that VAT is an invoice-based tax - or, put another way, a paper-pusher's paradise. Everything coming into the business has its input tax attached (it's a jargon-lover's paradise as well!), and the input tax has a tax invoice attached. The same is true of all the supplies by the business. Output tax must be charged on all taxable supplies, and a tax invoice issued as well. Your job is very simple - to keep track of every single tax invoice. More than this, you must by law keep a check on every supply made by your business, including all the exempt and zero-rated supplies.

Put that way, it sounds horrific. It is not easy to meet all the VAT requirements. But remember that a business which does not have proper and full records is inviting trouble in the longer term. VAT officials may be doing you a favour by forcing you to do this.

Where this level of bureaucracy (imposed or self-imposed) can become a burden is in the retail trade, but there are **Special Schemes** operating there which make for a simpler life. The other problem of an invoice-based tax is that you must account for tax charged on an invoice although your customer has not paid. This is tough on the smaller business, but the problem is now eased by the new **cash accounting scheme**.

Formal details of the special schemes available are given in VAT Notice 727, *Retail Schemes*. An explanation of each scheme is given in *Choosing Your Retail Scheme*, and details of each scheme are given in a series of *How to work...* pamphlets. If you are involved or intend to be involved in a retail trade, obtain these from your local VAT Office.

KEEPING RECORDS

SPECIAL SCHEMES FOR RETAILERS

There are 14 different schemes or variants of schemes designed to simplify the process of finding how much VAT your business is collecting and incurring. They have different turnover levels and therefore require different levels of detail. They also allow for your business making supplies of one or more than one kind. For example, Scheme C applies to small businesses which are supplying both zero-rated and standard-rated goods. Instead of invoicing every transaction, the supplier is allowed to work out the VAT by applying a standard mark-up, which is agreed with the VAT Office, to his or her purchases of standard-rated goods. She or he then only needs to keep the invoices for purchases, or till records. That example shows that retail schemes can save much time and any retailer should investigate them.

CASH ACCOUNTING

This is a recent simplification of VAT available to smaller businesses. Full details are contained in VAT Notice 731, *Cash Accounting*. Cash accounting can be used by any business which has taxable supplies of under £300,000, in any year, and which has its VAT affairs up to date. It does not apply if the business is using a retail scheme.

The cash accounting scheme allows businesses to get away from the practice of being treated as collecting and paying tax whenever invoices are issued (because of the rules on **tax point**). This can mean that the business is accounting to the VAT Office for tax not yet collected. To avoid this, the business is allowed to make returns based on tax on payments received less tax on payments made. This will be of advantage to any business suffering from slow payers and the occasional bad debt. It will not be of advantage to a business that pays more VAT than it collects. For example, this applies where most of the supplies are zero-rated. The cash accounting scheme does not cut down on the record-keeping.

Another scheme allows simpler bookkeeping. Businesses eligible for cash accounting may also qualify to make annual VAT returns instead of the usual quarterly returns. They must agree estimates of the amount of VAT payable with the local VAT Office, and then pay this in equal instalments over most of the year. The final payment, towards the end of the year, is adjusted to take account of the amount that is payable, rather than the estimate.

ANNUAL ACCOUNTING

VAT Offices are good at producing detailed guidance for those who have to operate VAT. Some of this guidance is compulsory - you must follow the details laid down, if it applies to you. This is usually set out in official Notices. Other guidance is to help and explain, in pamphlet form. If you are likely to be involved, get the leaflets relevant to your business, and at least follow *The VAT Guide* (Notice 7) - this is essential.

VAT INFORMATION

Those, and other leaflets on detailed topics are yours for the asking. There are lots more, for example on second hand ships and shoes, though not apparently sealing wax, cabbages or kings. They are all listed in *The VAT Guide*. For that reason, this chapter did not go into great detail, though it will pay you to do so.

5   *Expenses to be claimed*

*I*T IS VITAL, if you are not to pay too much tax or VAT, that you keep notes of your business expenses, and that you set all the expenses that you are entitled to deduct against your profits. Keep evidence, too, of those bills to prove they were incurred - and to remind yourself of your expenses. They may be larger than you imagined!

Income tax on a business is based on the **net profits** after taking into account all allowable expenses. If you do not have a full note of your expenses, you may be paying tax on an excessive level of profits. NI contributions on the self-employed are also based in part on the income tax accounts, so allow for the expenses as well. Equally, any liability to CGT depends on the gain made, not the total sales proceeds. Above all, VAT is based on tax collected less tax paid out. If you are registered for VAT and do not keep your bills, you will pay excess VAT to Customs.

Unfortunately, but not surprisingly, there are tax

rules that determine what expenses are allowable as deductions and what are not. Sometimes you may claim only part of your expense as a deduction. In other cases you will get none at all. Sometimes you will get an allowance for one kind of expense, but not for another. For example, you get the full cost of renting an office, but no allowance for buying one. This chapter examines (in alphabetical order) many kinds of expense you may incur, to see the position for each tax, including VAT. Before we do this, some general points need to be noted.

THE REAL COST OF
EXPENSES

When looking at business expenses, do not look at what you pay out but at the real cost of your expense after your taxes are paid - the **post-tax** position. The following example of Kit's carpets shows the difference.

WHAT'S DOES IT COST
AFTER TAX?

Kit, who is VAT registered and pays income tax and Class 4 NICs, decides to buy for £1,000, a new carpet for work and also, for another £1,000, a new carpet for the sitting-room at home.

Carpets are taxed under VAT at the standard rate of 17.5 per cent (rates correct at the time of writing), so the true price of both carpets is £851 plus VAT of £149. Kit can claim back the £149 VAT on the business carpet against the output tax but cannot get back the VAT on the sitting-room carpet.

The work carpet therefore costs £851 before VAT. Kit can claim an income tax deduction for the carpet, by way of capital allowances (see

Chapter 6) which will over time allow a full deduction of the cost of the carpet. The same thing will automatically happen for Class 4 contributions. Although not immediately, Kit gets the full cost of the carpet set off against profits. This saves income tax at 25 per cent (it might be 40 per cent) and NICs at 7.3 per cent (if tax is 40 per cent, there will be no NIC). Total saving is 32 per cent of the £851 (£275). The true cost of this carpet is therefore £576, or not much more than half the full-cost sitting room carpet. Still not cheap, but it does make a difference!

KEEP PROPER RECORDS

Of course, Kit cannot just make up the fact that the new work carpet was purchased. Kit must have bought the carpet. To show the tax authorities that expenses are properly claimed, you need effective records of what you spent, and when you spent it, as part of your accounts. As already noted, this is particularly important for VAT.

Income tax on profits - To be allowed, an expense must be:

> Of an income or revenue, not capital, nature
>
> Wholly and exclusively spent on the business
>
> Not expressly disallowed by law.

Expenses allowable to a landowner against rent are covered in Chapter 11. No expenses are allowed to individuals for investments and savings (such as shares or bank interest).

Capital gains tax - To be allowed, the expense must be a capital (not income or revenue) expense incurred on the item being disposed of, and of a kind expressly allowed by law. There is more detail on this in Chapter 6).

VAT - To be allowed as *input tax*, the VAT must have been paid on goods or services used for taxable business purposes, and not expressly disallowed by law (see also Chapter 4). Input tax is not allowable where the outputs, or business, is exempt (for example, finance, insurance, health, education). Where a business is partly taxable and partly exempt, only part of the input tax is allowed. In this chapter, for simplicity, we assume that the input tax has been incurred only for outputs which are taxed, including zero-rated supplies.

The income tax rule that expenses must have been 'wholly and exclusively' for the business is a strict one. It was designed to stop purely private expenses being set off against business profits. But, strictly, it also prevents expenses made partly for the business and partly private being set off as well. Take for example the clothes you wear for work. Unless they are a uniform or protective clothing, they are partly worn for work but also partly worn to keep you decent and warm. They are therefore not "wholly" for work, and so are not deductible. If you use your telephone both for work and private use, the rental will not strictly be allowable, only the cost of business calls. This is a strict rule.

TRYING IT ON

In practice the Revenue does not usually insist on the full extent of this strict attitude on most expenses. They will agree a reasonable split for, say, a telephone bill or car expenses, as we note below. But if you try making excessive claims or pushing your luck too hard, they may in turn claim to apply the law strictly - and you will lose out.

HOW THE REVENUE
CHECK

The Revenue approach to business accounts is necessarily somewhat selective. What they want are properly prepared accounts. Frequently, after a simple check for arithmetic, they will be accepted. If not satisfied (and in some random cases) they will ask for further evidence from your books and invoices. They can also make other checks on a statistical basis.

For the smallest businesses, the Revenue does not even want details of your expenses, just the totals. If you make gross profits of under £15,000 all they will expect is a three-line statement something like this:

Income from work as gardener   £6,800
Expenses   £   700

Profit   £6,100

For a small business, this tells them all they want to know. This is because one thing they watch is the mark-up of the business. They have available to them not just the accounts of your business, but also those of all your rivals. If they find that, say, one fish and chip shop seems to have heavy expenses and is only making 10 per cent profit, while all other fish and chip shops in the area are making 30 per cent profit or more, they will rightly be suspicious. They will probably check until they find some evidence to prove this heavy expenditure. (More seriously, they may also suspect that income is being understated, and investigate that, too). They also have powers to check with the VAT people about VAT returns. If the tax and VAT returns are found to be different, someone has some explaining to do!

VAT officers have three routine ways they can check your expenses. First, they make regular control visits, when they will both talk to you about your business and check your records. Second, they see both sides of any VAT expense. If you are claiming input tax, then someone should also be paying the tax. If they are not, or the two bills do not agree, then they obviously have reason to challenge the claim. The third aspect of VAT office checks is computer monitoring. Information from every VAT return is fed into the main VAT computer at Southend. If it does not like what it is being asked to swallow - for example a sudden large expense claim - it will blip. When it blips, officers tend to investigate.

HOW THE VAT OFFICES
CHECK

However, whether it is IT or VAT, you are fully entitled to deduct all proper expenses if you can prove them. Here are details of things you should be claiming.

64 KINDS OF EXPENSE

Note: under each head we look at the income tax (IT) rules, then any special VAT rules, next any special Capital Gains Tax (CGT) rules and finally capital allowances (CA) - further explained in Chapter 6.

Accountancy and audit fees - IT: allowable. Strictly, fees for tax compliance work by accountants are not allowable, but this point is normally ignored. Costs of tax appeals and tax planning advice are not allowable. VAT: input tax is deductible.

Advertising and publicity - IT: normally allowable. This is true even if you also intend someone else incidentally to benefit (as with ads in the church magazine or at the local football club). Permanent signs are capital - you may get a CA.

Bad debts - see **Debts**

Bank charges - IT: allowable on business accounts. See also **Interest**. VAT is not charged on finance charges.

Books and magazines - (Can you get the tax back on the book?) In practice, books and journals bought for the business may be allowed, although strictly magazines are a revenue expense and allowable, while books are capital, and eligible for a CA. This rule will apply if you buy a major work. There is no VAT on books or newspapers.

Business gifts - see **Entertainment**

Capital expenses - IT: not allowed as deductions, but CAs can be claimed. See Chapter 6. See also **Renewals**. Proper capital expense can be allowed for CGT. VAT: there is no distinction between capital and revenue expenses, so the input tax can be claimed unless disallowed expressly. See **Capital goods.**

Capital goods - VAT only: input tax on capital expenditure is allowed in full for all capital expenses except those caught by what are called the 'capital goods' rules. These apply only to large purchases of land or buildings (£250,000 or more) subject to VAT or large purchases of computer equipment (£50,000 or more). If you plan to spend sums like these, check the position, because you are only allowed to claim the input tax over a period of years.

Charity payments - IT: will be allowed if you make reasonable payments to charities in the interests of your business, but disallowed if for the benefit of the giver's family or not for the business. Both individuals and companies can separately claim tax relief for a **Covenant** to a charity. Companies (but not other traders) can deduct up to 3 per cent of their dividends for the year as allowable expenditure on a charity and a new relief, called Gift Aid allows deductions for single payments of £400 or more to a charity. All employers can operate a deduction system for their employees, so that employees may give up to £600 a year to charity free of tax. Businesses can also second staff to a charity and still claim a deduction for their pay.

Clothing for work - IT: 'smart' clothing for work is not allowable, even if you *only* wear it at work. If you need a uniform (evening suit for a musician or waiter) or special protective clothing (boiler suit, safety wear), this is allowable. VAT: protective clothing is not VATable where the wearer buys it.

Compensation and damages - IT: payment of

compensation or damages to a customer or after an accident from the business accounts is not usually deductible - unless the injury or damage occurred as part of the process of earning the business profits. The moral is to insure properly, as general **insurance premiums** are deductible if they relate to the business.

Computers - IT: these are capital equipment, for which CAs may be claimed, although peripheral items may be revenue. VAT : input tax deductible. However, it must be shown that the computers are used wholly for the business. If a visiting inspector asks you to turn your computer on, and finds its memory crammed full of games loaded on by your kids, expect to find some scepticism if you are claiming the whole of the input tax!

Covenants - IT: the cost of a deed of covenant to a charity is deductible against the total income of an individual or company, but not against the *business* profits. Covenants must be in the correct form and last four years or more in normal cases. Covenants have been used widely to cut tax on payments to students and after a divorce, and in some other cases. Most of these uses were stopped in 1988. See also **Charity payments**.

Debts - IT: usually accounts are based on money earned by the business even if not yet received. Debts are not allowable as deductions unless they become *bad debts*. This means that they remain unpaid after all reasonable attempts to collect have been made, or where the debtor is insolvent. A bad debt allowance is not allowable. When a bad debt is later paid, the debt must be added to the business income. Debt collecting costs are allowable. Debt collecting costs are allowable. VAT: the rules are more relaxed, and allow relief for any debt over six months old and written off by the trader. Both tax and VAT problems can be avoided if your accounts are on a **cash basis** rather than an **earnings basis**. See Chapters 3 and 4 about this.

Depreciation - IT: although all well-drawn accounts should allow for depreciation of the value of capital items, this is never allowable in tax accounts, or for CGT purposes. Instead, the profit may be reduced by any CAs allowable for plant and machinery, or other limited kinds of expense. See **Capital expenses** and Chapter 6.

Directors' fees - if the business is a company, directors' fees are allowable for corporation tax purposes, but there are special rules for tax and NI preventing the use of loans to directors avoiding this tax charge.

Dividends - if the business is a company, its profits are paid out to shareholders as dividends (unless already spent, eg on interest or directors' fees). Dividends are never allowable against profits for corporation tax purposes. When a company makes a dividend payment, it must also pay ACT to the Revenue (see Chapter 7).

Entertainment and business gifts - IT: most forms of business entertainment and gift are expressly disallowed as deductions against business (or employees') income. The only exceptions are costs of entertaining staff of the business, and small business gifts. But these must:

Cost £10 or less, incorporate a conspicuous ad for the business, and not be food, drink or tobacco; or

Be free gifts to the public generally made for advertising purposes; or

Be items normally supplied by the business in its trade (eg free samples).

VAT: input tax is not allowed for business entertainment. See also **Luxuries, amusements and entertainments**. Supplies of business gifts will normally be supplies in the course of business, and therefore taxable outputs on which VAT is payable. See also **Charity payments**.

Equipment - major pieces of equipment (such as a designer's drawing board or computer hardware) will be capital expenses and CAs will be available. Expendable equipment, or equipment with a short life, will be treated as allowable revenue expense - for example, pens, knives, machine ribbons, brushes, cups and saucers. See **Renewals**. VAT: input tax on all these items is deductible.

Finance charges - see also **Hire purchase, Interest**. IT : finance charges in addition to interest (for example, bank fees) are deductible unless they are treated as capital expenditure, as where the finance costs are charged to capital or incurred in relation to the purchase of capital items. VAT : finance charges are exempt from VAT.

Fines and penalties - IT: fines, penalties and related legal expenses are not deductible where incurred by the business owner, because they cannot be incurred for the purposes of the business if it is run properly. Payment by an employer of staff fines, such as a parking fine for a van driver, may be allowed. VAT : fines are not subject to VAT.

Fire safety - IT : equipment such as fire blankets or extinguishers is capital, and is subject to a claim for a CA. So also is any expenditure on meeting the conditions imposed for a fire safety certificate for any buildings used for the business. VAT : input tax is deductible.

Foreign travel expenses - IT: the costs of travel and living abroad for business purposes are allowed in full for the individual, but not for the family or for holidays taken during the trip. Deductible expenditure includes cost of accommodation, food and drink as well as travel. VAT : foreign VAT cannot be reclaimed against UK VAT liability.

Franchise fees - IT: this is not straightforward, because it depends what the franchise fees are for. Initial payments *may* be capital and not allowable, but if they are payments for services, eg training, they will be. The annual payments will partly be for services and use of copyright, and allowable. VAT : if the fees are subject to VAT, this is deductible as input tax.

Gifts - IT: gifts to employees are deductible if genuine work expenses but not if excessive. Free samples are also allowable, but for limits on other business gifts see **Entertainment**. VAT: gifts are supplies and therefore VATable.

Health costs - IT: medical bills, health insurance and other costs incurred on yourself are not allowable, even if they are incurred to save your business losing profits. Health costs of employees are, however, deductible. VAT is not payable as health supplies are exempt.

Heating, lighting, power - IT: allowable if incurred for the business. If the cost is for heating part of your home used for the business, a reasonable apportionment should be allowed. VAT is now payable on all heating bills, and input tax can be claimed where the heating is for business purposes.

Hire purchase, credit sale - IT: the cash price of goods, leaving out all VAT, is capital on which a CA can be claimed. A deduction can usually be claimed for the interest. The VAT incurred on the items purchased can be claimed as input tax. There will be no VAT on the finance charges.

Improvements to buildings and equipment - an improvement is work that makes a building or equipment better than when you first bought it. A repair brings it back to its original state or condition. IT: improvements are capital expendiiture and not allowable. (CA's may be available for equipment.) VAT: input tax is claimable.

Income tax and other taxes - IT: not surprisingly, you cannot deduct the cost of one tax bill against profits to reduce another tax bill, so income tax, CGT and corporation tax are not deductible from each other. **Rates** are deductible, as are **NI contributions** (but only for half of your own Class 4 contributions).

Insurance premiums - IT: premiums incurred for business purposes, eg insuring premises or staff, are deductible (and see **Compensation**). No VAT is payable. However, from 1994 a new insurance premium tax is being levied on all premiums. The cost of that tax is deductible with the premium.

Interest - IT: interest incurred by the business for business purposes (eg a general bank overdraft) is deductible, as is the cost of interest incurred by a partner borrowing money to buy into a partnership or buying equipment for the partnership. Other incidental costs of loans, such as commissions, are also deductible. See further **Finance Charges**. There is no VAT on interest.

Land and buildings - IT: the cost of buying land and buildings, or erecting a building is capital, and is not allowable. CAs are available for industrial buildings and agricultural buildings, but not for shops, offices, warehouses or private houses (with limited exceptions). See also **Rent**. VAT: this is complicated, and explained further in Chapter 11.

Leasing costs - costs of leasing equipment, for example a car, are normally deductible. See Chapter 6. VAT : Input tax is deductible.

Legal expenses - IT: allowable if spent on getting legal advice about something that is itself a revenue expense, eg collection of debts or entering a lease. Legal costs on capital items (eg setting up the business) and on non-business expenditure, eg where the owner is defending a drink-driving charge, are not allowable. Lawyers' fees are subject to VAT, which is deductible if the fees are.

Life assurance - IT: premiums for policies taken out on the life of a key employee (eg a top salesman) are deductible if the policy is short term (five years or less). Premiums for other policies are not deductible. VAT: insurance premiums are exempt, but are subject to the new insurance premium tax.

Loans - (see also **Interest**). The cost of a loan made by, but not repaid to, the business is only deductible if it is the practice of the business to make loans. This is true where someone is required to pay out on a guarantee of someone else's loan. The repayment of a loan or mortgage by the business is a capital payment and not deductible on the accounts, although it may be relevant to CGT. Incidental costs of loans, eg brokers' fees, are allowable.

Losses - see end of this chapter.

Luxuries, amusements and entertainments - In 1994 a new rule was introduced tightening up on VAT input tax claims for expenditure regarded as luxury items or as entertainment or amusement. For example, VAT officers are likely to challenge claims for input tax on the purchase of a racehorse or a motor cruiser under this rule. However, any expense is claimable if genuinely for business purposes, whether or not the goods are used by others as luxuries. IT: personal expenditure is not allowed, but again, if a luxury item is purchased solely for business purposes, it is deductible. See **Entertainment**.

Meals - IT: many people have tried to claim the costs of meals at work. They have failed. The cost of lunches at work (or claims for the extra costs of lunch away from home) is not allowable at all. Nor are meals provided as entertainment: see **Entertainment**. VAT: input tax is not deductible.

Motor vehicles and their running costs - the capital cost of a vehicle gives rise to a claim for a CA, although there are limits on the amount of CAs claimable for cars. The cost of leasing a car is deductible, as are the running costs such as petrol, repairs and servicing, insurance, licence (though employees may be taxable if you supply them with a car and free petrol or servicing). The sale of a car is exempt from CGT, though tax may be payable if other vehicles are sold at a profit.

VAT is payable by the business if it supplies its cars at a charge, if it sells cars at a profit, or if it supplies petrol for private motoring. As an anti-avoidance measure, if a sole trader supplies himself with petrol for private use, he must pay a scale charge, but can then claim the VAT on all petrol bought whether for business or private use. The scale figures vary from year to year, and on the size of the car, but are around £25 a month. If you spend less than about £50 a month on petrol, it will be cheaper not to claim the input tax on petrol at all, and avoid the scale charge. But check the right figures for your car and business.

NI contributions - IT: the cost of the employer's Class 1 contribution for any employee is deductible in full. Half the cost of Class 4 contributions of the self-employed is deductible, but Class 2 and Class 3 contributions cannot be deducted.

Pensions and pension contributions - IT: pensions payable to former staff and their families are allowable. It is normal to buy pensions through approved pension funds. Contributions to approved funds, both for yourself and for your staff are fully allowable. Further, the income of pension funds is tax free. You, and your staff, only get taxed when the pensions are paid.

Personal expenditure - IT: this is never deductible. VAT: input tax cannot be reclaimed on personal expenditure, although if something is bought partly for the business and partly for private use, an apportionment can be agreed.

Political contributions - IT: not deductible, unless (exceptionally) it can be shown that the cost is incurred for the purposes of business.

Postage, delivery charges, stationery - IT: allowable in full. VAT is not payable on postage costs, but is payable on delivery services.

Pre-trading expenses - see **Setting up the business**

Rates - IT: allowable on the business premises.

VAT is not levied on rates.

Renewals - IT: costs of renewals of small items of equipment or replacements of parts of capital equipment are allowable, though the original purchase was capital. VAT : input tax is deductible.

Rent - IT: allowable, although see **Land and buildings**. VAT: may be payable on commercial rents: see Chapter 11.

Repairs and improvements - IT: repairs to buildings and other assets are allowable expenses for income and corporation tax, although improvements to those assets are not allowable (except insofar as they make repairs unnecessary). Improvements which increase the value of the asset at the time of sale are deductible for CGT purposes. VAT is payable on repairs and alterations.

Research and development - IT: allowable under special provisions, though speculative, and whether revenue or capital, provided it is incurred for trading purposes.

Royalties - IT: payments of patent and copyright royalties are deductible. They are liable to VAT, so input tax is deductible.

Security - IT: burglar alarms and similar equipment is capital and CAs can be claimed. Revenue costs such as security staff will be allowable in full, as will rental of security equipment.

Setting up the business - IT: the initial costs of the business, eg legal fees, costs of setting up a company, interest on loans taken out before the business starts, travel costs and so forth are claimable under special provisions set out in Chapter 7. VAT: input tax can only be claimed from the time the business becomes registered for VAT, or such previous date as you and Customs may agree.

Social Security - see **NI contributions and Pensions**

Staff costs - IT: allowable in full, including all cash pay, provision of benefits in kind, pension contributions, NI employer's contributions, staff welfare costs, entertainment of staff (only), but not if the level of pay (eg to members of the family) is excessive for the work done. The Revenue has been known to argue that some staff costs are capital, for example, staff costs on capital developments. However, this will be exceptional. VAT: paying staff is not a supply, but making gifts in kind to them may be.

Subscriptions - IT: payments to trade associations and professional bodies are normally allowable. VAT is not usually payable on such payments.

Technical education - IT: the costs of a trader paying for a college to provide technical (but not general) education for employees are allowable - even if the employees are his own children. So is the cost of sending employees for re-training.

Telephone - IT: allowable if for business use. If the phone is used both for business and privately, the call charges and rental should be split. VAT: is payable on telephone bills.

Theft, and other crime - IT: the cost of stock losses and cash losses caused by criminal actions of staff and customers is allowable, but losses where, eg, a director or partner commits a major fraud on the business are not (though insurance premiums for insuring against such losses are allowable). Loss of capital assets through theft amounts to a disposal for CGT causing an allowable loss (unless the assets are insured, in which case they are treated as being sold for the insurance money. If the asset is replaced from the insurance money there is no charge). Damage to assets is treated as a part-disposal for CGT purposes (see Chapter 6), but money spent on repairing damage is allowable for income tax, and not deductible for CGT purposes.

Trading stock - IT: cost of purchase allowable in full. The cost (or value if lower) goes in each year's accounts (see Chapter 3). VAT payable on buying trading stock is fully recoverable against VAT on selling it.

Travel costs - IT: costs incurred exclusively for the business are allowable in full, including residential hotel bills, as is the cost of foreign travel. Taking your wife or husband with you is not allowable, unless it can be shown that this is also solely for business purposes. See also **Foreign travel expenses**.

VAT - IT: If you are a registered trader, leave all VAT out of your income tax accounts, both input tax and output tax. If you are not registered for VAT, all VAT you pay out should be included with the expenses.

Use of home as office - see Chapter 5.

TAX TREATMENT OF LOSSES

Where someone makes a loss rather than a profit, there will be no tax, because this is treated as being a profit of nothing. Fairness requires that the loss be set off against other profits, to stop the taxpayer being overtaxed in total, but this does not always happen. Different rules apply to different kinds of losses and different taxes.

If a taxpayer makes a loss from a trade or profession, **loss relief** is available. The loss can be set off against any other taxable income in the year in which the loss is made. Because most businesses run on the **preceding year basis** of accounts, that means the loss can be set off against the *previous* year's profits. It can also be set off against any other kind of taxable income that year of the taxpayer. If that does not provide enough of a cushion, it can be carried forward one year and set off against any income of the following year. The example shows how.

Sarah runs a small shop, which is usually quite profitable, but in the trading year 1993 she made a £10,000 loss. The accounts of her business are run on a calendar year basis.

Sarah's tax loss is treated as being made in the tax year 1993-94. In that year she would normally be taxed on the profits made from her shop in the calendar year 1992. So, for tax purposes, she can deduct the £10,000 loss against the 1992 profits before paying tax.

If the 1992 profits were less than £10,000 she would pay no tax on them, and could set off any unrelieved loss from 1993 against any other income she has.

In 1994-95, Sarah would normally be taxed on the 1993 trading profits. She will therefore pay no tax on her business that year.

Where this rule is not enough to allow full relief, the unallowed loss can be carried forward to set off against the next taxable profits of the business. Special rules apply to losses in the first years of a business, in the final years of a business (see Chapter 3), and when a business is turned into a company (see Chapter 7).

The effect of these rules taken together is that a taxpayer (or a partnership, or a company) can set tax losses from one trade against either profits on another trade, or against any other kind of earned or investment income. This provides some sort of cushion both against the lean periods of a business, and against starting in a risky business.

LOSSES ON INCOME FROM LAND

Losses on income from land (because revenue outgoings exceed the rent) cannot be set off generally against income. They can be set off against any past or future rent from that property under the lease or tenancy. Relief against other rented properties is only allowed under limited conditions if the landlord is running them properly for profit.

OTHER LOSSES FOR INCOME TAX PURPOSES

The general rule for other kinds of losses (eg Schedule D Case VI) is that they can only be set off against other income that year, or in the future against the same kind of income of the taxpayer. The system assumes that losses do not occur on investment income.

CAPITAL LOSSES

The rules for CGT (and capital losses, made by companies) are the same as the 'other' losses from income tax. Losses are worked out in the same way as gains (see Chapter 6). Any losses are set first against gains that year, with any excess losses being carried forward against future gains. Losses cannot be set off against

EXPENSES TO BE CLAIMED   99

trading or other income for income tax purposes.

If you have a VAT loss, you will have paid out more VAT on inputs than you have collected on outputs. This happens regularly in zero-rated trades. In any such case, you can claim the excess VAT back from the VAT Office. You should not be out of pocket at the end of the day. However, high claims for repayment of input tax are likely to trigger a control visit from a VAT officer. This will be to find out if the expenditure is properly incurred, and, perhaps, whether you are genuinely carrying on a business.

LOSSES AND VAT

6   *Taxing capital item*

....*AND CLAIMING* for them. In this chapter we discuss when claims can be made for capital expenses, and how CGT taxes capital profits on selling or disposing of capital items. There are special rules for both these problems, because income tax deals clumsily with business and personal assets. Perhaps we should feel sorry for the poor old thing. After all, it was invented during the Napoleonic wars, before anyone had thought of railways, companies, or electric lighting. In those days, business assets consisted of millwheels, carthorses and slaves on sugar plantations. Small wonder the rules don't really work on computers, satellites and milk quotas. Rules dealing with capital assets have had to be added on. This is not so with VAT. The difference between capital and revenue is normally irrelevant to VAT.

We will deal first with claims for allowances for capital expenditure. Very broadly, something counts as capital rather than revenue if it is going to last for some years. If it will have a useful life of less than two years, it will be revenue expenditure. If it will last more than five years, it will almost certainly be capital. In between things are not so clear. It depends on what is obtained for the money spent. A capital item is one that brings some lasting benefit to the business, and provides it with some asset. By contrast, items bought with a view to resale, and bills incurred to meet day-to-day expenses are not capital.

Accountants normally deal with capital expenditure by putting something for **depreciation** in the profit and loss account. This is not permitted for tax purposes. Relief from tax on capital items can be claimed only through **capital allowances.** Further, these are available for certain kinds of expense or investment only. Where there is no allowance, you can deduct nothing for the expense against your profits. Because of these limits on tax relief for capital items, it pays to think how you buy something in order to maximise the reliefs that are available.

Costs of new capital items, such as machines or new business premises, do not count against profits in the same way as revenue expenditure. There are two reasons for the refusal of the tax authorities to accept depreciation as stated in the accounts as a deduction for tax purposes. The first is because the law allows deductions only for some kinds of capital expense. In other cases it has been decided that no expense should be provided for. The second is because there is a standard rate of deduction for income tax purposes, while each accountant is free to choose individual rates of deduction for individual clients. The cost of a capital item counts for tax purposes only if the cost is for business purposes.

CAPITAL ALLOWANCES

WHAT EXPENSES CAN BE CLAIMED

Capital allowances are available only for the following types of expense:

Plant and machinery - this is very wide and covers all sorts of equipment. In practice it applies to all kinds of business.

Industrial buildings - such as a factory, but not a building used mainly for an office, shop, warehouse, or home, so this is chiefly important only to the manufacturing trades.

Specialised allowances - allowances are available to some special industries: for agricultural land and buildings, mines and quarries, dredging and the oil industry.

Research costs - research and development expenditure is allowable in full, whether the cost is revenue or capital.

Apart from these allowances, no deductions are available. For example, a retail business can claim allowances on the shop equipment (such as freezers or cash tills) but not the shop building.

PLANT AND MACHINERY

The words *plant* and *machinery* are taken from the tax laws, but they are not fully defined there. The words cover all forms of equipment (rather than buildings or the setting of the work) bought for any kind of business.

You must always show that the equipment was bought for the business. The legal test is the same as for general expenses: was it bought wholly and exclusively for the purposes of the business? However, unlike the rules discussed in the last chapter, apportionment is allowed if an item is used partly for business purposes and partly for private purposes. This applies both to the use of the equipment and the kind of equipment selected. If you use your car both for business and privately, you can claim capital allowances on a "just and reasonable" share. For example, if a newsagent decides, on winning the pools, to deliver his newspapers by Rolls Royce, the tax inspector is unlikely to accept that this choice of car is justified by the business. By contrast, an estate agent who gives customers a lift to properties in an expensive Porsche can show that he needs a good car to impress them.

You can claim a capital allowance for any of the following:

Advertising and publicity screens

Air conditioning, space heating and similar equipment

Alarms and security devices, including fire safety

Expenditure to meet Fire Brigade requirements and other safety equipment

Books, manuals, guides (but journals are revenue expenses)

Canteen or other amenity expense, eg cooking equipment and crockery (though replacements will be revenue expenses)

Carpets and other detachable floor covers, curtains, blinds

Cars, vans, lorries - even horses - if used for the business

Computer software and licensing costs
Cooling equipment

Cookers, refrigerators, and other kitchen and washing equipment

Counters, checkouts and display equipment for shops

Demolition costs for removing old equipment

Equipment of artists and craftsmen, such as looms, potter's wheels, kilns, drawing boards, musical instruments, disco equipment

Fees incurred directly in connection with acquiring new plant, eg engineers or architects' fees, but not fees related to financing the equipment such as interest charged to capital

Heating and air-conditioning equipment (but not mains services supplying them)

Installation costs of machinery, including costs of altering buildings

Lifts, elevators, cranes and similar equipment for lifting or transporting people or goods

Lighting equipment designed for display or to create an `atmosphere', eg in a restaurant, but not ordinary light fittings

Machinery for any industrial or commercial purpose

Movable office or shop partitions, counters and fittings (but not fixed screens or shop fronts which are part of the structure)

Office equipment - calculators, computers and their peripherals, typewriters, storage cabinets, dictation equipment, photocopiers

Office furniture - chairs, tables, cupboards, paintings, sculptures, murals, tapestries, prints, and other decorative assets where these are purchased to create `atmosphere' as in a hotel

Safes and similar security equipment

Telephone equipment, faxes, telex machines, including wiring

Thermal insulation, including costs of insulating buildings

"Plant and machinery" does not cover buildings or anything forming part of them (such as walls and permanent partitions, central heating ducts, mains electricity and water supplies, mains sewerage systems) or their grounds (such as roads, embankments, car parking spaces). Deciding whether something is part of the building or is equipment is complicated. The tax laws contain detailed provisions on this topic, key points of which are included in the account set out. If planning a new building, ensure your plans take full account of what is allowable.

A business that spends sums on plant and machinery in any year can deduct part of the cost in that year and in each future year until the full cost is met. The amount allowed each year is usually 25 per cent of the cost of the item as far as this has not been allowed in previous years. This is called a "reducing balance" allowance. The example in the box overleaf explains how this works.

HOW THE ALLOWANCE
OPERATES

BUYING EQUIPMENT :
THE CAPITAL ALLOWANCE

Kit buys a piece of equipment costing £1,000, for use in the business, and claims the 25 per cent allowance on it. (Note that if Kit is registered for VAT, the cost *excludes* the VAT. If Kit is not registered, then VAT should be *included* in the cost.)

Year 1:
Kit spent £1,000 and claims 25 per cent, so deducts £250 against the profits for income tax. This reduces the tax bill by £62.50 if Kit pays income tax at 25 per cent, and £100 if paying at 40 per cent.

(Separately, the capital allowance counts in working out profits for Class 4 NI contributions. Kit may therefore be able to offset the amount of the allowance against contribution liability at 7.3 per cent. This would reduce the total cost by a further £18.)

Year 2:
Kit has received allowances on £250 of the expenditure. This reduces the balance for claims in Year 2 to £750 (£1,000 less £250). Kit claims 25 per cent of this, a total of £137.50 (This will have values for income tax and NI contributions in the same way as in Year 1.)

Year 3:
The amount left over from last year (reducing balance) is £562.50 (£750 less £187.50). Kit claims 25 per cent of this, amounting to £140.62.

[and so on ...]

The table in the next box, below, is a `ready-reckoner' on the allowances year by year on an initial cost of £1,000.

ANNUAL CAPITAL ALLOWANCES
ON EQUIPMENT COSTING £1,000

Year 1	£250.00
Year 2	£187.50
Year 3	£140.63
Year 4	£105.47
Year 5	£ 79.10
Year 6	£ 59.33
Year 7	£ 44.50
Year 8	£ 33.37
Year 9	£ 25.03
Year 10	£ 18.77

The rules assume that assets normally last at least five years. In cases where the assets will have a shorter life, the business can receive allowances over the actual likely life of the item. To claim this, the owner must notify the tax authorities that he is claiming for a **short life asset**. The cost is then spread over the likely life of the item by the appropriate reducing balances.

In practice, equipment will often be replaced before it has worn out, and before the amount of the year's capital allowance is negligible. In addition, businesses will have several assets on which they are claiming allowances. How does this work?

SELLING OR SCRAPPING ASSETS

If a piece of equipment is taken out of use by the business, the owner may have claimed either too much capital allowance (because the asset is sold for a profit) or too little (because they scrapped the item, but have not had all the price allowed). To deal with this, the allowances are adjusted by a series of **balancing charges** and **balancing allowances**.

BALANCING CHARGES

A balancing charge operates when an item is sold for more than the amount of capital allowance unclaimed at the time of sale. For example, Kit sells the equipment that was bought for £1,000, after two years for £800. Kit has claimed allowances of £437.50 (£250 and £187.50), so has £562.50 unclaimed. But the sale price is £800, so there will be a balancing charge on her of £237.50 (£800 less £562.50).

The balancing charge is added to the profits of the business for the year. This increases the profits so the Revenue recovers the tax. In the example, Kit must pay more tax in Year 3 to make up for the excess allowances in Years 1 and 2.

A balancing allowance works the other way. For example, Kit scraps the £1,000, equipment in Year 2 because new technology has made it worthless. The scrap value is only £50, so there is a loss. Kit received £437.50 in allowances, but has spent £950 in total on the machine after recouping the scrap sale proceeds. Kit is therefore entitled to a balancing allowance of £512.50 (£950 less £437.50). This balancing allowance is an extra deduction against profits in Year 3 and will reduce Kit's tax bill.

Most businesses will have several items of plant and machinery on which they can claim capital allowances. In these cases, the different allowances are **pooled**, to use the jargon. This means that all reducing balance allowances from previous years are added together each year with all new claims for allowances, in a pool of expenditure. This pool is then adjusted for all balancing allowances and charges for the year. The adjusted amount is the sum on which capital allowances can be claimed for that year. The next example shows how this works, assuming Kit buys a new item costing £1,000 each year, and scraps the first item for £50 scrap value as just discussed.

POOLED ALLOWANCES

Year 1:
Item 1 bought for £1,000. Allowance £250 (see above)

Year 2 :
Item 2 bought for £1,000. Balance for item 1 is £750.
Pool is £1,000 for item 2 and £750 for item 1, total
£1,750.
Allowance for year 2 is £437.50

Year 3 :
Pool from previous year: £1,312.50 (£175 less
£437.50).
Add cost of item 3: £1,000.
Add balancing allowance on item 1 (scrapped for £50):
£512.50

Total pool now £2,825
Allowance £706.25.

Balance to Year 4 is £2,825 less £706.25

ALLOWANCES ON CARS

Restrictions operate on allowances for cars costing over £12,000. You cannot claim the 25 per cent allowance on more than £12,000 in any year. The total unallowed cost is carried forward and kept subject to this ceiling until the unallowed cost for a year is below £12,000. To let this happen, the cost of cars caught by this rule must be left out of the 'pooling' of allowances. You cannot sidestep this rule by leasing a car, because the same limit applies there. If you lease a higher-priced car, only a proportion of your leasing costs is allowable against tax (the proportion £12,000 bears to the total cost).

Special rules apply to the charge of capital gains tax (or corporation tax on chargeable gains of companies) on equipment on which a capital allowance is granted. These rules are designed to prevent a double allowance or charge to both income tax and CGT. When an item on which a capital allowance has been granted is sold, CGT is only charged if the sale proceeds exceed the original cost of the item. It is limited to the excess. This rarely arises, but when it does a charge to CGT can be avoided if the sale proceeds are reinvested in replacement equipment. Sale proceeds will usually be less than the original cost. That loss is not allowable for CGT purposes.

A business can acquire the use of business equipment in three main ways:

Outright purchase, either from its own resources or on an overdraft or loan facility. If a capital allowance is available, it can be claimed when the asset is acquired. Any interest is deductible against trading profits.

Leasing. This does not involve buying the item at all. Consequently, no capital allowance can be claimed. Instead, the full cost of leasing rentals is allowable against profits if the asset is used exclusively for the business. The leasing company will usually be claiming a capital allowance for its purchase of the item. A lessee can benefit from the tax relief indirectly in the leasing rates charged. If there is a final capital payment, or balloon payment, at the end, that may not be allowable.

Hire purchase, credit sale or other instalment

purchase schemes. Here the buyer pays the seller or finance company for the item and for interest on borrowing the outstanding amount, plus any fixed charges. The buyer is treated for capital allowance purposes as buying the item outright at the date of the agreement, and then paying the interest and charges separately. Any capital allowance can be claimed from the date of the agreement, although the asset is not bought until later. The buyer then claims a deduction against profits for the interest when paid, deducting any fixed charges in the first year.

PLANNING PURCHASES WISELY

You can see that these are genuine choices. Which should you choose, and what other points should you watch so that you do not pay too much tax? There are two key differences between leasing and the other alternatives. First, the full cost of leasing is deductible against tax. Assuming that you make a profit and pay tax, the deduction makes the real cost of leasing significantly cheaper than the cash rental. It is still not cheap because there is a hidden finance cost in it, so get comparative figures before deciding this way. Second, leased assets do not appear on the balance sheet of the business, because you do not own them. This is often referred to as **off-balance sheet finance**. It reduces the assets of your business, which is sometimes an advantage, sometimes not.

Buying from your own resources often looks the cheapest option - but it is only superficially so. Work out what else you could be doing with the money. If it could earn more elsewhere, you lose those earnings while buying the equipment. Take a simple example. I intend to buy a car with my savings. It will cost £10,000. My savings are currently on long term deposit earning 7 per cent interest before tax. If I buy the car, I will be losing income of £700 a year before tax (rather less when the tax is deducted). If I keep the car for one year it may well lose, say, £2,000, in value. I have therefore lost not only £700 this year, but at least £140 every year on this year's depreciation of the car. Could I have done better - should I buy a cheaper car?

TIME IT RIGHT

Plan when it is best to buy. You get the same capital allowances granted at the same time on your purchase whether you buy at the start of the accounting year or at the end. The later in the accounting period you buy, the quicker you get some of your money back. That's not advice to delay - it's advice to think ahead, with perhaps an eye to buying at the end of the previous year. This is so particularly if you're buying on hire purchase, or with any sort of interest holiday (that is, free credit period before you start paying interest). An agreement signed just before the end of a year has an advantage over one signed just a little later.

Watch the VAT as well. If you are registered for VAT, you are entitled to get the **input tax** on your purchases back. You can do this only by setting them against your **output tax** at the end of each return period. It is therefore best to pay a bill involving a significant amount of VAT as near the end of the return period as possible. But if the equipment is going to earn you money, it is not worth waiting for that reason alone. It may be better to bring the **tax point** forward to an earlier account period, by arranging quick delivery or early invoicing, even if the cost is still met later. If you are not registered, but you are going to incur heavy expenses followed by profits later, consider voluntary registration. This allows you to reclaim the VAT you will pay on equipment.

BUILDINGS AND WORKSHOPS

For the costs of buildings, a highly advantageous special allowance operates alongside a rather ungenerous main rule. First, the full cost of a wide range of buildings in **Enterprise Zones** can be set off against income tax straight away. This is a most generous allowance for capital cost and explains why so much new building takes place in these zones.

The general rule is that expenditure on buildings and land does not qualify for any allowances at all. This is because buying land and most kinds of building is regarded as an investment that will pay a handsome profit in the long run. Meanwhile it will save the owner significant rent costs. This is not true of factories. Like equipment, they tend to wear out. Some kinds of industrial building therefore get a limited relief.

INDUSTRIAL BUILDINGS

You can claim limited relief on any building if you incur capital expenditure on buying or constructing a building or structure. This is provided that the building is used only for a trade involving:

Manufacturing, processing or stockholding goods

A mill or factory or similar buildings

Mining, agriculture and some other special trades

To qualify, at least 75 per cent of the building must be used for that purpose. Buildings used as offices, private houses, shops, warehouses, garages or any other purpose not covered do not qualify unless they form part of an industrial building but less than a quarter of it. This is why the caretaker's house and the factory shop are often part of the main building. Besides industrial buildings, capital allowances are also available for hotels and for sports pavilions used for employees.

The allowance is a deduction against profits for tax purposes of 4 per cent of the original capital cost each year for 25 years. If the building is sold, let on a long lease, or taken out of industrial use during that time, there will be a balancing charge or allowance like those for plant and machinery.

The key idea of CGT is very simple indeed:

CAPITAL GAINS TAX

If you have	**Assets**
Which you	**Change**
So you	**Gain**
You pay	**Tax**

In other words, if when you dispose of any capital item you show a profit, you are liable to CGT on the gain, unless you are entitled to some relief.

CGT taxes all kinds of property unless the particular item is exempt. It potentially covers anything you can sell or make money out of - even rights to sue someone, rights to share in someone else's profits or an employment contract. Business assets that will be caught include:

Land and buildings, and any interest in land, such as a lease or advertising rights

Investments such as shares, debentures, some forms of government stock (National Savings and some government stocks are exempted)

Machinery and equipment worth over £3,000 and sold at more than the purchase price

Rights under contracts, and to take legal actions against others

Valuable objects such as paintings, antique furniture, valuable books, unless held by the owner as stock in trade (eg for an antiques business)

Goodwill on a business

An important issue is to know what's exempted from the tax. The main exemptions are:

Your only or main home - but only if you use it all as a home. If you use any part of it *exclusively* for your business, or for letting, you risk losing part of the exemption. Always use your house partly for living in, if only at weekends

Cars, but not vans

Objects worth less than £3,000, when you dispose of them. If you try to break up a set to cut the value of the parts below £3,000 that won't work. It's the full set that counts. This rule does not apply to land, or to investments such as shares

Things with an expected life of under 50 years when you get them, other than items used in a trade. This removes most household items

Money in sterling - but not profits or losses made on foreign currencies

Debts, that is, the right to receive money at some future time; but this does not cover secured debts such as mortgages, debentures and government stock

Life assurance policies held by the original owner. This is to prevent tax being charged when the policy is paid up

Insurance policies where the item insured is not itself a chargeable item (eg personal injuries insurance). Where the insurance is of, say, a building which is chargeable, and a claim is made, the building is, in effect, treated as sold for the insurance proceeds. The loss on the building is cancelled by the gain under the policy

Trading stock. This is because trading stock gets fully taxed by income tax. This rule also applies to anything else where the profit or loss on a sale is taken into the income tax accounts

DISPOSAL

There is a liability to tax, or a right to claim a tax deduction, whenever a taxable asset is disposed of to make a gain or a loss. `Disposal' means any kind of transfer from a person of her or his rights to it. For example it covers all sales, leases, mortgages, exchanges, gifts or the loss or destruction of an item. There is a disposal whenever part of an asset is disposed of or a capital sum is derived in some way from an asset. For example, part sales of land include selling off part of the land, selling a lease over the land, or selling someone the right to park cars on part of it or to extract minerals from it. What it really comes to is that if you have a taxable item, and you make a capital sum out of it, CGT will apply unless one of the exceptions operates.

Important exceptions to tax include charities and gifts to charities; pension funds; employee trusts; heritage property, and trusts and bodies looking after the national heritage (such as famous works of art and stately homes, universities and libraries).

BUSINESS GIFTS NOT TAXABLE

Transfers between husband and wife do not attract tax. More generally, if the giver of a gift of business assets and its receiver agree, they can jointly notify the Tax Inspector that they want to postpone the CGT that would otherwise be payable when the gift was made.

Under the normal rules, a gift (or a sale at a deliberately low value made non-commercially) is treated as a sale at the market value of the item given. CGT is payable if that produces a gain. If the giver and receiver choose, they can treat the receiver as getting the gift at the price paid by the giver. For example, if Kit decides to pass business assets on to another member of the family as a gift (or for a nominal amount), then the beneficiary of Kit's gift will be treated as acquiring the assets at the price Kit paid for them. This holds true, whatever their actual value at the time of the gift. If the family member sells the assets, tax will be payable on the whole rise since Kit received them.

A potentially damaging charge to CGT could arise if a business sold one of its assets with the intention of replacing it. For example, Kit sells a shop in Ambridge with the intention of buying one in Brookside. Under the usual rules, CGT is payable on the sale of the shop, leaving less money to plough back into the new business.

ROLLOVER RELIEF ON BUSINESS ASSETS

A `rollover relief' exists to prevent this happening. If you sell a business asset, but use the proceeds within a period starting 12 months before the sale and ending 3 years after the sale to buy a replacement asset of the same kind, then any gain made on the sale is `rolled over' on to the new asset. This is done by reducing the cost of buying the new item for CGT purposes from the price you paid for the new asset by the amount of the gain made on the old asset. When you finally sell up, tax will be payable on both sales.

Because of rollover reliefs on business assets, and gifts on which tax is postponed, much of the CGT payable during the life of a business can be postponed. Until when? Usually, the rollover stops when the owner sells up and retires. This leaves a potentially heavy charge hanging over the business when someone gets older, just when they want to take money out to sort out their retirement. To avoid this charge being too heavy, a special relief operates, as explained in Chapter 10.

WORKING OUT GAINS
AND LOSSES

If the sale proceeds exceed the deductible expenses, there is a **chargeable gain.** On the other hand - and just as important - if the expenses exceed the proceeds, there is an **allowable loss**. Losses are calculated in the same way as gains. Loss relief is described in Chapter 6.

The sale proceeds are treated as being the amount actually received if the disposal was a commercial one. In other cases, as with gifts or sales between relatives, the market value of the items at the time of disposal are treated as being received as sale proceeds. This applies where the asset was bought or acquired since 6 April 1982.

ONLY NEW GAINS
TAXABLE

CGT is only chargeable on gains made since 6 April 1982 (or 1 April in the case of companies). Where an asset was owned on 5 April 1982 some of the gain made on a disposal will relate to the time the asset was held before that date. If the item has been held for a long time, much of the gain might therefore be outside the taxable period. How is this handled? The main rule is that the item is treated as being bought on 5 April (or 31 March) at its market value on that date. This will sometimes require the expert guess of a valuer. The value at that date is treated as the purchase price, and the gain worked out against it.

This is dealt with partly in Chapter 5. For CGT, only expenses of the following kinds are deductible:

Purchase costs, or costs of making the item (or the price on 5 April/31 March 1982 if the asset was owned then)

Incidental costs of purchase (legal fees, surveyors' fees)

Costs of enhancing the value of the asset, reflected in the value at sale (but not running repairs)

Costs of protecting the asset, for example, legal costs of fighting a claim by someone else to ownership

Incidental costs of sale, eg estate agents' fees, advertising costs.

Keep records of all capital expenditure, and of the purchase price of capital items whether acquired before or after March 1982, together with details of all costs of selling the assets. This will make accurate claims for allowable expenses much easier. If a cost is deductible for income tax, it is not also deductible for CGT.

One trouble with CGT is that it taxes cash gains, rather than real gains. That is, it taxes the inevitable rise in values caused by inflation along with the actual gains in real terms. To avoid that, an **indexation allowance** is added to each item of expense. It is the amount by which the cost of living has gone up since the expense was incurred (or on the value at March 1982 if later) up to the month in which the sale took

ALLOWABLE EXPENSES

INDEXATION
ALLOWANCE

place. The Revenue regularly publishes tables of these allowances. They are reprinted in most tax journals and are available in most good libraries.

THE RATES OF CGT

CGT is charged on the total taxable gains in any income tax year, that is, the net amount of gains less losses for the year. The first £5,800 (in 1994-95 - the figure is usually revived every year) is free of CGT; the rest gets charged as if the top part of income for income tax purposes, at 25 per cent, then 40 per cent (or at the corporation tax rate for the company).

Let's tie all this together with an example:

Our old friend Kit bought a shop as a going concern back in 1973, and sold it in June 1993 also as a going concern. The sale price was £90,000 for the freehold of the shop and goodwill, with stock at valuation. Kit paid £10,000 in 1973 (aside from the stock), and it is estimated that the market value was £60,000 in 1982.

For CGT purposes we ignore the stock, as that is included in the income tax calculations. If the sale price included fixtures, we must divide it to isolate any sums paid for exempt assets, and also for equipment on which capital allowances have been paid (as these are ignored for CGT purposes).

Kit's sale price was £90,000, but there will have been lawyers' fees, estate agents' fees, stamp duty and other selling costs. Let's say they totalled £4,000. Kit bought the shop in 1973. This is before the 'base" of the tax in 1982, so instead we need the market value at March 1982. The total value was £60,000 then. Kit has had no capital expenses on the shop since 1982 (that's to keep it simple - in reality there would probably have been some allowable expenditure on improvements).

What gain did Kit make? To find that out, we must first find out the indexation allowance from March 1982 to June 1993. In the tables it is (we'll say) 0.400. Kit's allowable expenses are increased by that amount, that is, the £60,000 value of the shop in 1982 is increased by 0.4, bringing it up to £84,000.

The sale proceeds less expenses came to £86,000. The chargeable gain is therefore £86,000 less £84,000 or £2,000. Kit will potentially pay tax on that at either 25 per cent or 40 per cent. However, Kit is entitled to £5,800 gains free of CGT each year. Unless Kit has other gains, no tax will therefore be paid. In any event, if Kit buys another shop to replace the one sold, that tax can be postponed until the new shop is sold. If Kit is over 55 and disposing of the business after running it for a long time, then retirement relief will be available. It is therefore unlikely that Kit will pay any CGT.

7   *Should I form a company?*

*I*T MAY BE, as Oscar Wilde said in *The Importance of Being Earnest,* that in married life three's company and two none. In business, two, or even one, can be a company, but that does not make it a good idea. Before you rush off to set up your business as the United Metropolitan Improved Punctual Delivery Company Limited, or whatever, a word of warning. It may cost you more in tax to form a company than if you leave your business unincorporated. It needs close thought. That's what this chapter is about.

Whether it is an advantage for tax reasons to be a company rather than a partnership or a sole trader is just part of the story. The status of a company may be of sufficient value to offset the extra costs. We look at these points in a special chapter in *Running Your Own Business,* and do not cover the same ground here. That chapter also looks at **partnerships**. A partnership is when two or more individuals (or companies) carry on business in common with a view to profit. Again, we do not repeat here what the other book covers. We look at taxation of partnerships briefly at the end of the chapter.

WHY COMPANIES ARE IMPORTANT

The key legal point about running a business through a company is that it is legally separate from you. Let's say you are running your own small business, and you want to set up a company to run it for you. You will, presumably, sell your business to the company. In exchange, you will become the main shareholder in the company. Afterwards, you will go on handling the business for the company. You will be its managing director. Therefore, you are no longer self-employed. The company is boss, and you are on its payroll.

CORPORATION TAX

As we have seen, British companies cannot pay income tax or CGT, but must pay corporation tax. There are some important differences between CT (as we call it for short) and income tax and CGT - particularly the rates. The current rates are set out in the box attached. The highest rate of CT is less than income tax or CGT, while the rate on a small company is the same as the lower rate of income tax. Times of payment and some other details are different. However the key rules, about how big the profits of the business are, and what expenses can be deducted, are almost the same. Where they differ, they tend to be slightly more generous to companies.

RATES OF CORPORATION TAX: 1994-95

Main rate of tax .... 33 per cent
(Paid by companies with profits over £1,500,000)

Small companies rate .... 25 per cent
(The small companies rate is payable by companies with total profits under £300,000)

Rate on profits between £300,000 and £1,500,000......................... 35per cent
(25 per cent is payable on profits below £300,000)

WHAT KIND OF COMPANY?

For tax purposes, there are two main kinds of companies. More common are: **trading companies**, which carry on some selling or servicing business. The others are **investment companies**, or holding companies, which are used as `vehicles' to hold property or shares in other companies. Companies are frequently operated in **groups**, with one or more holding companies holding the shares in separate trading companies. There are special rules for handling the taxation of groups of companies. They are designed to treat the group as if it were one company or person. This works both for CT and for VAT, but details of the rules are beyond the scope of this book.

Of course, a trading company may have investments and investment income, and a holding company may in part be involved in a trade, but the two kinds of income are best kept apart. In particular, there are special anti-avoidance tax rules aimed at small companies with investment income. The problem is that a company can be used just to save tax on investments. The company will pay tax on the income at the CT rate. It will not pay income out to its owners, so they will avoid the higher rate of income tax. Because of this, the law provides that small closely-controlled investment companies must pay CT at the full rate, not the 25 per cent rate whatever their size. There are also other rules cutting down on tax advantages of these companies. This does not, however, apply to trading income, with which we are chiefly concerned in this book.

On the other hand, an investment company may deduct its expenses of management when calculating its tax, where an individual cannot. Anyone wishing to handle investments on any scale through a company should keep the arrangements separate from his or her business, and obtain separate advice about it.

The profits of a trading company are calculated for CT purposes in just the same way as profits of an individual are calculated for income tax, except:

TAXING A TRADING COMPANY

Interest payments - companies can deduct all interest payments against profits before calculating the amount of tax. (They are known as "charges on income".) This replaces, and is wider than, the individual's mortgage relief.

Charity payments - the company can deduct payments under covenants as charges on income, and also a total of 3 per cent of the income distributed as dividends.

Capital gains - gains on disposals are worked out in the same way as for CGT, but the amount is added to the total of taxable profits when working out how much CT is payable, and charged at that rate.

Dividends - companies pay profits to their shareholders as dividends or distributions. When they do so they must pay **ACT** (advance corporation tax) as explained below. They cannot deduct the cost of dividends against profits (unlike interest on loans).

Payment of tax - this is always paid at the latest 9 months after the end of the accounts year.

PAYING MONEY OUT
OF COMPANIES

A company running a business must be registered for **VAT** separately from its owners, if the level of turnover of the company is over the levels requiring registration (see Chapter 4).

Profits earned by a company are the property of the company, not of its owners or employees, and the company pays tax on these profits. How are those profits paid to the owners? For the smallest companies, there are usually just a few people who own the company by owning all the shares. The owners will often also be the directors of the business and its employees. They may also provide working capital to the business by way of loans. And they can wind the company up at any time if they so choose. How the profits are paid to them will reflect these ways of controlling the company.

There are four ways the money can be paid out. First, this can be as **earnings** to the directors or employees - either in cash or by benefits in kind. Either way, the company can deduct the cost of the pay and benefits in working out its taxable profits, if the payments are made for work actually done. The company will operate the **PAYE** scheme and pay the earnings with tax deducted. It will also pay NI contributions on behalf of the employees, including the employer's contribution.

Secondly, the money can be paid out as **interest** on loans made to the company. This will be appropriate if the owners choose to limit the amount of money they put in by buying shares, and provide extra capital in the form of loans. Again, interest is deductible against profits for tax purposes. When the company pays out the interest, it must deduct basic rate tax and account to the tax authorities for it.

Next, the money can be paid out as **dividends** on the shares. When this happens, the company has to account for **ACT** to the tax authorities. As we see below, this is the equivalent of deducting lower rate tax.

Finally, the money can be paid out as a **cash payment** to shareholders **on winding up** the company. When taxpayers receive money in this way for their shares, they are treated as selling them. There is a disposal for CGT purposes. They will therefore pay tax at the basic or higher rates of income tax on any gain made as part of this "sale".

Apart from a winding-up (when the company is lost), basic rate tax or lower rate tax is therefore deducted on each of these. Does it matter how payment is made? As between interest and dividends, the importance is that money tied up in shares is less flexible than money tied up in loans. It can be arranged that the interest paid on the loans is related to profits, making it much like a dividend. It is easier to alter loan arrangements than to alter share capital. Sometimes it is therefore worth exploring the use of loans rather than shares to finance a company. Expert advice should, however, be taken in these cases. The lender should certainly also take advice.

If the owner is paid earnings, more tax may be payable. This is because the earner, and the company, must both pay NI contributions on earnings. Even on higher earnings the company must still pay standard rate NI contributions (currently at 10.2 per cent). The earner gets a pension in due course, but if the earner has already paid maximum NICs, the extra contributions will add nothing.

ACT AND TAXES ON
DIVIDENDS

When a company pays a dividend to shareholders, it must also pay ACT (Advance Corporation Tax) to the Revenue. The rate of ACT is currently 25 per cent. This means that if the company pays out, say, £80 as a dividend it must pay 25 per cent of this, £20, to the tax authorities. To pay out a dividend of £80 the company must therefore have £100 available. Looked at the other way, the dividend is paid to the shareholder as £80 plus a tax certificate for £20. The shareholder is treated as receiving a total payment of £100, with the lower rate tax of £20 paid.

This system must be operated whenever a company pays out money to shareholders, except on a winding-up or paying back share capital. It is there so that the government receives tax when dividends are paid out to meet the tax due from shareholders. At the same time, the ACT is, as its name indicates, an advance on the tax due from the company. If you think that this is double counting, you are right. It is. The idea is to stop excess levels of tax by taxing the company on profits and the shareholder on those same profits when paid out as dividends.

Note that, as part of this, the main income tax rate on dividends and similar payments is the 20 per cent lower rate of tax, not the 25 per cent basic rate. If the taxpayer has income over the level for paying higher rate tax, then the higher rate (currently 40 per cent) is also payable on the top part of the income.

To make ACT work, the company must provide the shareholder with a **certificate of deduction**, similar to that in the box below:

WIBBLE WIDGETS LTD

DIVIDEND AND TAX CREDIT

I hereby certify that Wibble Widgets Ltd paid to (William Wibble) the dividend stated below on 31st. March 19** in respect of ordinary shares for the year ending on 31st. March 19**.

Amount of dividend (.................)
Tax credit   (.................)

I further certify that advance corporation tax of an amount equal to the sum shown above as the tax credit will be accounted for to the Collector of Taxes.

31 March 19**
Kit Fothering, company secretary

Unlike interest or earnings, dividends cannot be deducted from profits for tax purposes by a company. Instead, for the reasons already mentioned, the company treats the ACT as an advance payment of its CT bill, both on income profits and capital gains. As the rate of tax on a small company is 25 per cent, the effect of this is to cancel most of the tax liability.

The resulting tax liability, if a small company hands out all its profits as dividends, is an effective rate of tax *on the company* of about 6 per cent. This is not so for larger companies, where the effective rate is about 16 per cent.

TAX ON SALES OF SHARES

The ACT system is designed to avoid double taxation of company profits. This would happen if the company pays tax on the profits. Then the shareholder pays another slice of tax on those profits when they are paid out as dividends, if there is no tax relief.

Double taxation does occur on capital gains of companies. If a company makes a gain, it pays tax at its CT rate. The rest of the gain goes to increase the company's assets, and therefore the value of its shares. If the shareholder sells the shares, he or she will pay tax (at 25 or 40 per cent) on the gain made in selling the shares, including the gains already taxed. This also happens if the company is wound up. The effect is double tax.

For example, a small company pays tax at 25 per cent. Its shareholders pay tax at 40 per cent. £100 gain to the company will leave £75 in assets. Assuming that gain is reflected in the company's shares, and all the shares are then sold, the £75 share value will get taxed at 40 per cent, which costs £30. This leaves only £45 of the £100 in the shareholders' hands. To make matters worse, a **stamp duty** is payable on all sales of shares. The duty is 0.5 per cent of the total value of the shares. It can be avoided if the shares are transferred by a gift or on death.

This double taxation is a problem in transferring a business from a company to individuals, or winding up the company. Once a business has been transferred to a company, it can be expensive to get it back out. This should be remembered when considering putting the business into a company.

There is also a risk of a charge to capital gains tax when a business is transferred by individuals to a company. This is because they are treated as disposing of the business to the company at its market value. That often causes a potential but substantial CGT bill on the individuals. It can be avoided only if the whole business (excluding only cash) is transferred to the company, and the price is paid by the company by issuing its shares to the individuals.

TRANSFERRING A
BUSINESS TO A
COMPANY

Not all tax can be avoided in this way. One problem is that the rollover relief from CGT on replacing business property (see Chapter 6) ends, forcing tax to be paid on bills that were earlier postponed. There is also a risk where a loss-making business is transferred to a company that the tax relief on losses may be lost. It can be carried forward under a special provision, but only if the transfer is wholly or mainly in exchange for shares in the business. In this case, it pays to get professional advice before making irreversible moves that may prove too expensive. There is no one answer to the question whether it is better for tax reasons to run a small business through a company. The checklist emphasises key points.

CHECKLIST:
TAX ON COMPANIES AND INDIVIDUALS

Tax rate on profits: CT rate on small businesses is 25 per cent up to £300,000, while individuals pay 40 per cent over about £25,000. Trading income can be held by the company, so the 40 per cent rate does not have to be paid until paid as dividends.

Tax rate on gains: same tax rates as income, <u>but</u> tax gets paid by both company and by individuals on gains, commonly making the total rate over 50 per cent. The double charge does not arise until shares are sold, or the company is wound up.

Time of payment: companies pay tax as ACT on paying dividends, and in any event 9 months after the tax year. Individuals can pay much later than that (although this advantage is being reduced - see chapter 12).

Stamp duty: payable at 0.5 per cent on sales of shares, but not usually on business assets (other than land).

Earnings of owners: if owners receive money as earnings, NI contributions are payable as well as PAYE tax, which noticeably increases its cost. Earnings are available for use in paying tax-free pension contributions.

Special reliefs: reliefs on retirement or death, or for gifts of shares in a family company and of a business are much the same. However, it is easier to transfer parts of a business as shares, so companies ease problems of estate planning for inheritance tax.

Partnerships do not exist as separate entities, but yet cause some of the worst business tax problems there are. How come? In England and Wales (but not for the wiser Scots) the law says that partnerships do not have any separate identity - there are only the partners. Income tax is therefore payable by partners as individuals on trading or professional profits of the partnership. Each partner is fully liable for all the tax due from the partnership in that year.

What causes the real problems is the **preceding year rule** (see Chapter 3). This year's partners get taxed on last year's profits. But what happens if the partners have changed? Or if the partners' profit shares have changed? Or if one partner is paying tax at 40 per cent while the others are paying at 25 per cent? The Revenue's answer is simple - it doesn't really care as long as someone pays the tax due. That leaves the partners arguing about who pays what share of the tax bill. That's not easy. If you are likely to run into that problem, get expert advice. The problem will ease when the preceding year rule goes, but will still be awkward.

A NOTE ON
PARTNERSHIPS

8   *Taxing the staff*

*I*F YOU RUN your business through a company your "staff" includes you. You probably have other staff, whether or not your business is a company. This may include your wife or husband paid to help you part-time, if only to take advantage of available tax allowances. This chapter examines how staff are taxed, whether managing director or part-timer, to see the difference tax rules may make in the way people are paid. It does so from the point of view of the employer. Full details are covered in my separate book on *Don't Pay Too Much Tax If You Are An Employee*.

WHAT TAXES APPLY?

Two must be watched :

Income tax as it applies to earnings
(**Schedule E**)

NICs paid by employees and directors
(**Classes 1 and 1A**)

WHO ARE THE STAFF?

That sounds a daft question. Don't you know who you employ? Well, maybe not, and with good reason. There's a knotty legal problem we need to look at. It's the answer to the question "what's the difference between being employed and being self-employed ?"

One way out of problems about staff is not to have any. OK, you need work doing, but you get it all done on sub-contracts. There are sound management and cost reasons for using self-employed sub-contract labour, leaving tax totally out of account. For tax reasons, sub-contract labour is often easier and may look cheaper. Some people therefore try to get all their 'staff' treated as sub-contract. It does not always work.

EMPLOYED OR SELF-EMPLOYED?

The difference is stated by lawyers as the distinction between a **contract of service** and a **contract for services**. Whether a particular contract is *of* service or *for* services depends on all the facts and circumstances, and not just the bits a written document includes. The key issue is the relationship between the individual and business involved. There must be some form of agreement if there is to be a contract of service. How the DSS and its agencies look at this is set out in the box.

A WORKS FOR B; IS A EMPLOYED BY B?

The DSS looks at the following pointers as indicating A is **employed** by B :

A is required to give personal service to B, for which A is paid

A is part and parcel of B's business

A is subject to B's control or right of control as to what is done and when and how it is done

B has the right to select, suspend or dismiss A.

The following indicate A is **not employed** by B :

A is not required to do the job personally

A is paid by the job, rather than on an hourly or weekly basis

A is in business independently, with B having little or no right to dictate hours or methods of work

B is not concerned whether or not A is making a profit.

PROBLEM AREAS

The vagueness of the test makes it inevitable that there are areas of dispute. The DSS and Inland Revenue have both been pushing for some time to get the groups of people who are regarded as employees expanded, and to cut down on those who are regarded as self-employed, especially in some areas (such as television staff, musicians and teachers) and where a lot of part-timers work. Their reasons are obvious - to get PAYE working, and to get higher contributions. By contrast, VAT officers look for the self-employed, because employees cannot be registered persons in respect of their employments.

Just to confuse things further, each set of tax officials make their own minds up about the status of a taxpayer. It can therefore happen that the Revenue regard someone as self-employed, while the DSS and the VAT people regard the same person as employed. The DSS make it worse by having rules (called **Categorisation Regulations**) which decide the status of some borderline cases - but they don't apply to the Revenue or VAT Office. However, in cases where those rules do not apply, the DSS and Revenue try and agree a common approach.

DSS CATEGORISATION REGULATIONS

A husband (or wife) can employ his wife (or her husband) as an employee to help with his or her work, but the wife (or husband) cannot be self-employed for this purpose. If the employment is for any other reason (such as to do 'his' housework) this is totally ignored, and there is no employment

Agency workers and 'temps' are regarded as being employed by their agencies

Office and commercial cleaners are regarded as being employed by whoever pays them, whether the business is where the cleaner works or an agency

INCOME TAX ON
EMPLOYEES

The rules charging income tax on employees and directors (known as **Schedule E)** catch the full amount of earnings from all employments, less only limited expenses. No problem normally arises with payments in cash. In practice, a wide number of fringe benefits are commonly paid, to save tax. These are caught in different ways, and it is important for employers to note the best way of paying their employees. This is discussed in detail in my other book, *Don't Pay Too Much Tax If You Are An Employee.*

NIC'S ON EMPLOYEES

These work under different rules to Schedule E. Liability on an employee's (or director's) earnings is to **Class 1 contributions**, payable by both employees and employers. There is little problem with cash payments. However, the rules for deciding what is "cash" are not consistent between income tax and NI contributions. There is also a special class - **Class 1A** - applying to employers who provide their employees with company cars. Otherwise, there are no NICs on benefits in kind or provision of accommodation or meals. Consequently, once it is decided whether a person is or is not an employee, there are limited disputes about contribution liability.

CLASS 1
CONTRIBUTIONS

There are several rates of Class 1 NICs. There is a minimum weekly earnings figure below which no contribution is payable, either by employee or employer. In 1994-95 this is **£57.00**. Above that figure, both employers and employees are liable to pay contributions under **Class 1** of the NI contribution structure. There is a **primary** contribution payable by the employee, and a **secondary** contribution payable by the employer.

Depending on both the overall weekly earnings of the employee, and his or her status, a set percentage of earnings (including those below the minimum) is collected from both the employee and employer. Details are in the rate box below.

NIC CLASS 1 RATES 1994-95

No contributions are payable where the weekly earnings are below £57.00

Where earnings are £57.00 or above, the **employee** pays :

> 2 per cent on the first £57 (£1.14 a week) and
> 10 per cent on the earnings above £57 up to a weekly maximum of £430

Where earnings are above £57, the **employer** pays :

> 3.6 per cent on all earnings up to £100
> 5.6 per cent on all earnings up to £145
> 7.6 per cent on all earnings up to £200
> 10.2 per cent on all earnings above £200
> (no upper limit)

Where the employment is **contracted-out**, the rates on employees are 1.8 per cent lower, and the rates on employers (below £430) are 3 per cent lower

Special low rates apply to certain married women and widows entitled to pay at a reduced rate (but not their employers)

Those over state retirement age (65 for men, 60 for women) pay no contribution, but their employers pay the normal rates

COMPANY DIRECTORS
AND NI

There are special rules for the NI contribution liability of company directors. These are designed to prevent you playing around with the way directors are paid (for example by means of loans rather than earnings) to avoid NICs. Full details are set out in DSS leaflet NI 39, *Company Directors and NI*. One practical point - see Chapter 5 - is that directors of small companies are usually also shareholders and can be paid either earnings or dividends. Payment of dividends saves no income tax, but it does save NICs, and is therefore worth considering in some cases.

THE BEST WAY TO PAY

There are savings for both employer and employee in the way the staff are paid. The example below should give you an idea of how.

Sue and Kate both want new dresses costing £100. Kate has to buy hers, while Sue can get hers from her employer, as she works in a dress shop. Kate buys hers at full cost out of taxed income. At 1994-95 rates, she is probably paying income tax at 25 per cent and NICs at 10 per cent. To earn the £100 net to spend on the dress, she must earn £154.

Sue earns a bit less than Kate, but gets other benefits. She can buy clothing at cost from her employer. This has a hidden VAT saving in it as well as the direct saving on the retail margin. Sue's employer sells her the dress she wants for £50 (costing her £77 in earnings). She gets the same dress as Kate, but earns £77 less to get it. Does her employer lose out ? Not as much as at first sight. If he pays Sue a bit less than Kate, he will be saving the employer's NIC on her pay (at 7.6 per cent or 10.2 per cent). He can still claim the cost of the dress in full against his profits for tax, and some VAT may be saved. And it may actually increase his sales!

Sue's employer could go a stage further, by insisting that Sue wore certain of his products whilst at work, and supplying them to her free on loan. Unless she is higher-paid, she pays no tax on a loan. The employer will of course want his staff to look good in a dress shop to maximise business. If the employer does that, Sue pays nothing for the dress. She may be very happy to wear such good clothes, particularly if she is £77 better off than Kate. There is also no NIC on supplying a dress for Sue's use.

What of VAT ? If the dress is used only for work purposes, there is no VAT to pay, because there is no supply. If it is used sometimes by Sue for private use, the employer should account for VAT, according to the rules, by dividing the cost of supplying the dress to her, after allowing for what it is still worth, between its use at work and its private use. That will probably not be much.

This is a simple example, but shows how the reinforcing of income tax, NICs and VAT mean that a bit of sensible planning allows employers to provide more value to employees at lower cost. It depends on the way that income tax and NI contributions are applied to employees' benefits. This is covered in full detail in Don't Pay Too Much Tax If You Are An Employee.

PENSIONS AND
CONTRACTED-OUT NICS

Pensions are a major point to consider, whether paying yourself as director, paying your wife as explained below, or paying any other staff. Apart from the compulsory NI contributions, you do not, of course, have to contribute to a pension plan at all, either on behalf of yourself or anybody else, but the tax concessions make pension plans the most effective way of preparing for your future retirement. Current legislation allows individuals to contribute a certain percentage of their earnings (up to certain maximum levels) to a pension plan and the tax benefits mean that both the contributions, and the funds into which they are invested, have no liability to income tax or to capital gains tax.

For your staff, you can either set up an occupational pension scheme or encourage them to take out their own personal pension plans. Their long-term financial plans are important and a considered approach can be useful in recruiting and retaining staff. As a director, there are other options open to you for your own pension; in all cases, pensions are an area where you will need good professional advice.

People with no occupational or personal pension plan will have to depend on the state pensions alone and these will simply not be enough. Although many employees will have the benefit of the State Earnings Related Pensions Scheme (SERPS) in addition to the basic 'old age' pension the government is increasingly encouraging people to rely less on state pensions (principally by reducing their value) and to make their own personal plans. It is now possible to leave SERPS ('**contract out**')provided it is replaced by an alternative arrangement. This will result in lower NI contributions (as set out in the box on p.141), though the reduction will be balanced out to some extent by the contributions to the alternative plan. Contracting out is only going to be beneficial to people under the age of 45 and it is another area where competent advice is required.

The swift answer is: hardly any, aside from pension contributions. No expenses are allowed at all against NI contribution liability, though this is offset by the rule that benefits in kind and an employer's contribution to a pension fund are not within the NI contribution net. The rules are much tougher than those applying to the self-employed.

In many cases where a husband is self-employed, his wife is not working. He can therefore pay her for helping him, so as to use up the wife's earned income relief, and the band of pay on which no NI contributions are payable - currently about £57 a week. This can be further supplemented by tax-free benefits. For example, if the husband pays contributions to a non-contributory personal pension for the wife, this will be a deductible cost for the husband's business, but not be taxable to the wife (or incur NI contributions), subject to premium limits. Had the wife not been paid anything, the pension contributions would not be permissible as deductions. The key issue is whether the cost to the husband's business is justified by the work the wife puts in. She must be doing something to earn her pay.

COLLECTING THE TAXES

Nearly all tax on earnings is collected by employers through the **PAYE** system, or Pay As You Earn. This covers both income tax and the NI contributions.

If you are employing anyone with earnings of over £57 a week (or any earnings at all from you, if total earnings from you and others are over that total), inform the Inland Revenue and your local Social Security Office (see Chapter 2). They will separately send you full details of how to run the PAYE system.

You will need to keep accurate records for anyone you are paying within the scope of the PAYE deduction scheme, including:

The employee's name

The employee's NI number

The employee's tax code

Dates of all payments

Amounts of all payments (and running totals of amounts through each tax year)

Amounts of any occupational pensions contributions

Amounts of any statutory sick pay or statutory maternity pay

Amounts of any sums given to charity under payroll-giving

Amounts of tax deducted (and running totals of amounts through   each tax year)

Amounts of NI contributions deducted

Amounts of employer's NI contributions payable.

This list shows that you must keep full records of all payments to staff and deductions collected from them to comply with the legal requirements of the PAYE system. To help you do this both the Revenue and the DSS provide standard deduction working sheets and forms, supported by explanatory booklets and deduction tables showing how much to deduct in any week or month.

The PAYE system requires all employers to make monthly returns (accompanied by a cheque for tax collected) to the Revenue. This return covers both tax and NICs, and the Revenue pass the NIC cash on to the DSS. A full annual return is also required.

Both the Revenue and the DSS are entitled to send inspectors to your offices to check these books without notice and at any reasonable time. You can be fined for not keeping proper records, and for not producing them or providing the authorities with appropriate information if they ask for it. What is more, they can still collect the tax from you that you should have collected from your staff - even if you did not in fact collect it.

AN INSPECTOR AT
THE DOOR

Ask your local tax inspector or DSS office if you want further guidance now. The following guides are available free : Employers Guide to PAYE (Leaflet P7) plus deduction working sheets and deductions tables; Thinking of taking someone on? PAYE for employers (leaflet IR53); Tax : Employed or self-employed? (leaflet IR56) - all from tax offices, and Employers Guide to NI Contributions (leaflet NP15); NI and contract of service (leaflet NI 39); NI for company directors (leaflet NI 35) - all from Social Security Offices.

9   *NI ins and outs*

T HIS CHAPTER is about two social security systems - the state's and yours, and what you pay and what you get. Many self-employed find the state system inadequate for their needs. That's why they need their own. The tax system can help in giving tax relief if you decide to provide for your own financial security - tax relief not just to you but also to the funds into which your money goes. (If your business is run by a company you are not self-employed - see Chapter 7).

WHAT YOU MUST
CONTRIBUTE

The self-employed must make two kinds of NI contribution :

Class 2 contributions - flat-rate weekly contributions payable if you are ordinarily self-employed, regardless of whether you actually do any work in any one week. The contributions are not compulsory for people with low earnings.

Class 4 contributions - an extra levy on income tax payable on trading and professional income (Schedule D Cases I and II to be technical).

Income tax is payable by people regardless of age. Not so NICs. If you are under 16 or over retirement age (65 men, 60 women), you don't pay contributions. Ask your Social Security Office for a certificate confirming you are not liable to pay, and send it to your tax inspector. You don't have to pay contributions, even though you have trading income, if you are not actively engaged in the trade. For example, a **sleeping partner** in a partnership, who is only investing in a business run by the partnership, is not self-employed, so does not have to pay NICs.

NICS FOR THE SELF-EMPLOYED: 1994-95 RATES

Class 2 :   £ 5.65 a week
Contributions are not compulsory for those earning under £3,200 in the year

Class 4 :   7.3 per cent of total trading and professional income exceeding £6,490, up to a limit of £22,360 in the year.

CLASS 2
CONTRIBUTIONS

These must be paid by direct debit from your bank to the DSS. For details of *Direct Debit - The Easy Way To Pay!*, as the DSS publicity puts it, get a copy of the leaflet with that title (leaflet NI.255) from your local social security office. It has Form CF 351 attached, which is what you need to set a direct debit arrangement going. That way you pay about the middle of each month.

EXEMPTIONS FOR LOW
EARNERS

If your total earnings from self-employment are likely to be below the threshold figure for the year, you don't have to pay Class 2 NICs, but you may do so if you wish. Why pay when you don't have to ? Class 2 contributions give a right to some benefits, particularly basic retirement pension and sickness benefit. If you don't pay, you will have a deficient contribution record, and may lose benefit. So you save now but may lose later. Check your benefit entitlements before deciding which to do. If you do choose not to pay, you need form CF 10, which you will find attached to DSS leaflet NI.27A, *People With Small Earnings From Self-Employment.*

CLASS 4
CONTRIBUTIONS

These carry no benefit entitlement. Nor is there any option about paying them. They are collected by the Inland Revenue along with the tax on your trading and professional income. There is a relief available against income tax. You can deduct half the cost of your Class 4 contributions against your profits for income tax purposes (though not of course in calculating your profits for Class 4 purposes). This rule does not apply to Class 2 NICs.

If you are one of the growing number of people

who are both an employee and self-employed, you may be required to pay Class 1 NICs as an employee as well as Class 2 and Class 4. If your earnings from both sources are high enough, this may result in you paying too many contributions, as there is an annual ceiling on the total amount of NICs any one individual is expected to pay.

The rules provide that you should not pay more Class 2 NICs than are needed to bring the total of both your Class 1 and your Class 2 NICs up to the maximum Class 1 contribution payable by you that year. They also provide a lower maximum for Class 4 contributions, so that you don't pay Class 4 NICs if you are paying in total under Classes 1, 2 and 4 more than the annual total of Class 2 and Class 4 together.

The annual maximums are adjusted each year, and you cannot always tell if you will pay too much. If you think your income may involve you paying too much, apply to the Contributions Agency for deferment of your Class 4 (and Class 2) liability. To do this, get form CF 359 which is attached to DSS leaflet NP.18, *Class 4 NI Contributions*, and send it to the Contributions Agency, Class 4 Group, in Newcastle upon Tyne.

Contributions paid late (that is, after the end of the week or year in which they should be paid) may suffer the penalty of losing the contributor some benefit entitlement, and also having to be paid at the rate set when they are paid rather than when they were due. The DSS have powers to enforce payment of unpaid contributions, partly by prosecuting people for not contributing and partly by civil procedures. Further details, and time limits for using late paid contributions for benefit entitlement, are included in DSS leaflet NI.48, *NI Unpaid And Late Paid Contributions.*

WHAT YOU CAN CLAIM

Class 2 NICs entitle you (or, if you die, your widow) to :

Sickness benefit - payable weekly when you are incapable of work because of an illness or disability. Many self-employed people do not know they are entitled to this. To claim it, you must be off work completely and, if away from work for more than a week, you also need a doctor's sick note. You can use the back of that as a claim form. You cannot, in any event, claim benefit for the first 3 days of any period off work through illness. If claiming sickness benefit, you need not pay NICs for any full week of sickness. Instead, you are credited with a contribution. That also applies to the next two benefits.

Invalidity benefit. Sickness benefit is available for only 6 months. After that, the long-term sick can claim the long-term weekly invalidity benefit for as long as they remain unable to work because of sickness, without paying any further NICs. (The government intends to replace both sickness and invalidity benefit with a new incapacity benefit in 1995.)

Maternity allowance - payable weekly to mothers expecting a baby or just after the baby is born, for a period of up to 18 weeks when they are off work. Details are set out in DSS leaflet FB 8, *Babies and benefits.*

Retirement pension - self-employed contributors get only the basic weekly retirement pension, not the earnings-related supplements. The basic pension can be claimed by anyone over 65 (male) or 60 (female) who has retired from work, but not by those taking early retirement. Full entitlement to the basic rate pension only goes to those who have paid full Class 2 contributions (don't forget that Class 4 contributions don't count) for roughly 9 in every 10 years of their full working life. If your contribution record is not this good, you may get a lower weekly pension. Further details are contained in leaflet NP. 32, *Your Retirement Pension*, from the DSS.

The full story for many pensioners receiving basic rate pensions only, even those with a full contribution record, must include entitlement to **income support** (the non-contributory supplementary income benefit) **housing benefit** (designed to help pay rent, but means-tested).and **council tax benefit**. This is because the basic rate of retirement pension is below the official poverty level for many claimants. Details of these benefits are beyond the scope of this book. They aim to provide only the minimum level of support.

For details of the retirement benefits, get leaflet FB 6, *Retiring?*, from your local Social Security Office. If you are getting near retirement and have a deficient contribution record (for example, because of periods when you were neither employed nor self-employed), you can sometimes pay voluntary contributions known as **Class 3 contributions** (at a little less than the level of Class 2 contributions for each week) to improve your contribution record, and therefore your pension. It's always worth asking.

> **Widow's benefits** - Class 2 NICs may also qualify a widow for the £1,000 **Widow's Payment** when her husband dies, and for **Widowed Mother's Allowance** and **Widow's Pension** on a weekly basis for widows left looking after children, or over the required age limit for payment of NIC's.. These benefits are payable at a flat rate, subject to certain conditions. For further details get leaflet FB 29, *Help When Someone Dies.*

BENEFITS WHEN STARTING IN SELF-EMPLOYMENT

Many people decide to start their own business because they are unemployed. If that applies to you, you should be receiving either **unemployment benefit** (which is payable weekly for the first year of unemployment) or **income support** (if you have been unemployed for over a year, or if you were not entitled to unemployment benefit because, for example, you had not paid enough NICs). The problem is that you will probably be subject to the 'available for work' rule, and you will certainly be subject to the £2 a day earnings rule. These say that you must be available for work at all times, and you must not be earning £2 a day on any day when you claim to be unemployed.

BENEFITS FOR LOW EARNERS

Again, if you are just starting in your business, and earning only a small amount - or your business hits a rough patch because, for example, someone is ill - do not forget you may become entitled to the **income-related benefits** even though you are still working. There are three benefits which can help the low income self-employed :

Income support - payable to anyone not in full-time employment or self-employment (defined as working for 16 or more hours a week)

Family credit - payable to anyone who is working over 16 hours a week, but has a family (that is, at least one child under 18 living with her or him) and a low income

Housing benefit - helps people with low or no incomes to pay their rent (either to the local council or to a private landlord)

Council Tax Benefit may also be available

The rules for all these benefits are pitched mainly at those unemployed or those who are employees, but there are special rules to take account of the position of the self-employed. If your income is low, and you think you might be entitled to claim, find out more by asking for advice from your local Citizen's Advice Bureau or, if there is one, a local Welfare Rights Centre or Law Centre. All these advisers are trained to deal with social security matters. Don't be one of those who does not ask for, and therefore does not get, their entitlement. It is believed there are many thousands of self-employed people who are entitled, particularly, to family credit, but who don't claim it because they don't know about it.

First, the bad news. Retirement pensions are not very good and are getting steadily worse. That's not intended as a political statement, it's a fact of life which no political party of any kind can wish away. The reason is simple, and all around you. There are fewer younger people entering the job

PLANNING YOUR OWN
FUTURE BENEFITS

market, and there are more people retiring and living to a considerable age.

The arithmetic of that is unavoidable, and affects every one of us. There will be fewer people around working, and they will have to pay more out to pensioners. This is because the state NI fund is not an accumulated fund - it is a pay-as-you-go scheme with hardly any capital behind it. That, inevitably, means two things. Contribution rates will rise, and benefits will be cut. Both have been going on steadily over the last 15 years, and will go on happening. Whether you are planning to retire in the near future or far future, take steps to protect your own position and that of the family whilst you can afford to do so.

TAX HELP IN PLANNING

There is an additional reason why you should plan ahead. If you invest your income in the right way you will get help in the shape of tax reliefs from the government to assist you in doing so.

You cannot afford it? That is a common reaction. The truth is that you cannot afford not to, if you have any reasonable level of income at all and you plan, as I do, to retire. After all, you are paying other people's pension contributions every time you buy a train ticket or pay your rates. So why not yours?

There has for many years been tax help for the self-employed in building up provision for retirement or - and you need to think of this too - benefits for the widow and family left when someone dies. Ask yourself this question if you have a family - what would they live on if you were killed this morning? They may be entitled to the benefits listed above, but is that good enough? And don't put off the answer. An old friend and neighbour of mine died without warning just recently - not that much older than me. What is your answer? Then do something about it.

Help comes in the form of a **personal pension** for yourself and your dependents. A personal pension scheme must be in a form approved by the tax authorities, but in practice standard schemes offered by the main companies will be approved. Tax relief comes two ways: an allowed deduction by you of premiums against your profits before tax, and an exemption of the funds of the pension company from either income tax or CGT (or their corporation tax equivalents) whilst the funds are held for you. You pay tax only when you draw the pension. Even then, you can receive a tax-free lump sum instead of part of your pension.

PERSONAL PENSIONS

The amount of tax relief you can claim against your profits depends on your age. The maximum is as follows :

TAX RELIEF FOR
PREMIUMS

Age	Percentage of income
Up to 50	up to 25 per cent
51-55	30 per cent
56-60	35 per cent
61 or older	40 per cent

That relief can be claimed each year, but can also be set off against earlier income if you did not claim the full benefit in the previous year. Experts agree that when you are near to retirement, you should be using your allowance as fully as you can afford, including unused allowances from past years.

You can also claim,as part of the total, a deduction of up to 5 per cent of your profits for a scheme to provide benefits for your dependants (your husband or wife, and your dependent children) on your death.

GET THE EXPERTS IN

Pension contributions are a trade-off: income now or income then. How you should best make that trade-off is a matter on which you should seek advice. Get the experts in. Ask pension and insurance companies, or brokers, for some quotes and examples of the ways in which you could be planning ahead. If your business is worth quite a bit, you should be planning this along with other plans to deal with retirement and tax. We deal with that in Chapter 10.

Because of these, and other, rules, people starting in self-employment find they lose benefit whilst not earning anything (or hardly anything) from the new business. If you are in danger of being caught in this position because you intend to start off on your own, apply to your Jobcentre for an **Enterprise Allowance**.

ENTERPRISE
ALLOWANCE

This is a weekly allowance (currently £40 a week) payable in place of unemployment benefit or income support to people starting on their own. Husbands and wives can both claim separately. Get full details from your local Jobcentre. You must meet the following conditions to be entitled to the benefit :

You intend to work full-time at a new business, and

You have not started that business yet, but

You have been unemployed for at least 13 weeks, and

You are receiving either unemployment benefit or income support, and

You are over 17 but under 60 (female) or 65 (male), and

You can produce a business plan and a viable business idea.

If you qualify, see the staff of the Local Enterprise Agency for your area or, if you are under 25, the staff of the local office of the Prince's Youth Business Trust, for advice. They may also be able to help you raise the starting capital. Who they are, and why you should see them, is explained in *Running Your Own Business*. If you do not know where to find them, pick up a phone and ask the operator for FREEFONE ENTERPRISE. It will cost you nothing, but the operator will put you through to the nearest office of the Training and Enterprise Council. They will tell you what to do and where to go.

10 *On retirement*

WHAT IS RETIREMENT AGE for the self-employed? One or two people I know managed to retire before the age of 40, at least for the first time. The oldest person was well over 90 when he stopped going into the office regularly. In both cases they were enjoying to the full the privilege of the self-employed of working on their own terms. Yet too many people struggle on in self-employment long after they wanted to retire, because they could not afford to do so, and had not planned ahead. Can you afford to retire on the right terms?

TAXING YOUR LIFE'S WORK

If your business has been at all successful, you will have built up a reasonable amount of capital, and it will probably still be tied up in the business. When you retire, you may want to free some capital. If you do, work out the tax position. Whether you sell the business, or just parts of it, or give it away to members of the family, there will be tax consequences. We must therefore look at each of the ways you could hand the business on, and the tax effect of doing so.

At some point, of course, the property must be handed on. It will happen to all of us, later or sooner. I was once asked to give an after-dinner talk to a professional audience about why they should get their wills written right. I queried twice whether they really wanted to talk about that after dinner, and was assured they did. I could not, and still cannot, find any jokes to lighten the burden of such a task. I wasn't thanked then for explaining a few home truths, and I don't expect to be thanked now. But spell them out I must. Far too many people put off sorting out their affairs, some of them for too long. Don't be one of them.

LEAVING THE BUSINESS

If you are a **sole trader**, when you leave the business, the business - at least for tax purposes - ends. That is so whether you sell it, give it away or close it down. Tax consequences of ending your business need planning like any other aspect of your business.

By contrast, if your business is owned by a **company**, you are only the owner of shares and an employee of the business. When you leave the business, it continues. It is only when the company goes out of business that the business ends.

Between those two is the position of the **partnership.** If you are in business with one or more partners, the business can come to an end every time the partnership changes. However, you can choose (provided all partners agree) that it does not end. That may be a practical solution to the problem, and many partnerships use it. But first, let's see the problem.

INCOME TAX WHEN THE
BUSINESS ENDS

The profit charged to income tax in the year in which a business ends is not worked out on the usual **preceding year basis**. Instead, tax is based on the profits (or loss) actually made in the **income tax year** in which the business ends. That is, the profits (or loss) are worked out from 6 April to the date on which you leave the business.

The changes to the preceding year rule that we discussed in Chapter 3 will also affect what happens when a business comes to an end. Under the rules for existing businesses, a gap appears between the accounts taken into account in the last full year of the business, and the year in which it ends. To deal with this gap, the Revenue (but not you) may change the basis of taxing the last two full years of business on to an actual profit basis. This means they can demand that you pay tax on the actual profits from 6 April two years before the end of the business, until the date on which it ended, rather than the normal basis. They will do this if that increases the tax. Because they probably did not know when the business was going to end until after it had ended, they will raise the new tax bill after it has finished. That bill must still be paid. Once businesses are on the new current year rules, the large gap disappears.

FINAL LOSSES

If the business ends making losses, the taxpayer runs the danger of losing the right to set the tax **losses** against profits. If that happens, then too much tax will be paid over the life of the business. To stop this causing too much injustice, there is a special tax relief. This allows traders to carry losses made in the last 12 months of business back up to three years. For example, a business ending in 1995 can carry its losses back to profits since 1992 if necessary. It can then claim a tax rebate to set off against those losses.

Another issue to be sorted out is what happens to capital allowances. Each item of **plant and machinery**, **industrial building** or other asset on which allowances have been granted must be reassessed and made subject to a **balancing charge** or **balancing allowance**. What happens depends on what is done with the plant. If sold, there may be extra tax to pay as a balancing allowance if the amount made selling the equipment exceeds the unallowed tax relief for buying it. If scrapped, there will probably be a balancing allowance. If used privately (for example, the business van becomes the family car) it will be treated as being sold at its market value. This also happens if it is given away. That may result in a balancing charge.

Trading stock must be valued at open market value at close. This may be higher than the value used in the accounts till then (which may be lower of cost and market). Any profit element 'hidden' in the stock will now bear tax. If stock is turned over to private use, it is treated as being sold at market value. If disposed of cheap in a closing sale, the proceeds will be the market value.

OTHER INCOME TAX
PROBLEMS AT CLOSE

PAYING VAT WHEN THE
BUSINESS ENDS

The VAT rules make it clear that you are running your business for VAT purposes even when you are disposing of it. A sale or gift of business equipment is a **supply** of goods. It must bear standard-rate VAT when that is appropriate, although it is in effect a sale of part of the business. Further, the sale or gift of the business as a going concern is expressly made a supply in the course of the business, and is therefore VATable.

Once you have sold or disposed of the business, you must deregister, unless you are carrying on, or intend to carry on, another business that will also bring you into the scope of registration. Notice must be given within 30 days of the business ending.

Remember that you have to account to the VAT Office for all VAT. If you are one of those managing to keep a cash-float in the business based on VAT collected and not yet paid to Customs and Excise, that will also come to an end.

TAXING THE SALE

If you sell the business or its assets, there is a potential **capital gains tax** charge on top of the income tax and VAT. The sale will be a disposal for CGT purposes, so you need to work out the gain. As we saw in Chapter 6, that gain is made larger because any **rollover reliefs** you have also end. This is because where you postponed paying tax on assets sold and replaced during the life of the business, the value of the new asset was reduced, possibly back to 1982 values.

CGT applies to sale proceeds of land and buildings, goodwill, industrial or intellectual property (such as sale of a trade mark), and any other assets except wasting and exempt assets. Remember that plant and machinery on which you received capital allowances is included only if you sell at above the original cost price. When that happens you cannot claim losses on their sale. But you may have rollover relief on those assets and end with CGT gains though real losses.

If, when all is added together, you show a profit (and, tax apart, I hope you do!), you must pay CGT unless retirement relief helps you out.

CGT RETIREMENT RELIEF

If you are over 55 when you sell the business (or part of it, but not separate assets, (or, if under 55, are retiring because of ill health), check how far the retirement relief can help. If you worked full-time with the business, and it is your business or one owned by a company of which you own some of the shares, there is a generous level of relief. At maximum, this removes entirely the CGT on the first £250,000 of gains, and reduces to half the tax payable on the rest up to £1,000,000. The maximum is available when you have owned the assets (or been involved in the business full-time) for at least 10 years. If you sell at 54, or if you fail to meet the requirements, you will lose all or part of that valuable relief. More details are set out in the box overleaf, so keep an eye on them.

GETTING RELIEF FROM CAPITAL GAINS TAX ON RETIREMENT

You must be:

> 55 or over, or
>
> Have retired on grounds of ill health

and be disposing of:

> The business, or
>
> Shares in the company owning the business

If you **own the business direct**, you must have done so for at least one year before selling (when you will get 10 per cent of the maximum relief). You must have owned it for ten years to get full relief.

If you are a **partner in a partnership running the business**, and you retire from the partnership, you can claim relief as if your partnership interest was a business asset.

If your business is **owned by a family company** (or group of companies) which is a trading company (or group), you can claim the relief if:

> You have been a full-time working director of the company, and
>
> The company is one where you have 5 per cent or more of the voting power

There are complex provisions dealing with groups of companies and family trusts. Here you need expert advice.

If you make a gift of business assets of a business carried on by you or of shares in your family company that is a trading company, and retirement relief is not available, you can still postpone a charge to tax on the gift. The relief will also apply if you sell the business at an undervalue. Relief is granted by treating the disposal as happening on a **no-gain/no-loss** basis. The effect is that the recipient receives the gift not at market value, but at the no-gain/no-loss value (ie what you paid for the assets or the value at which you were given them). The relief must be claimed by both you and the person receiving the assets.

PASSING ON THE
BUSINESS BY GIFT

If you sell land (or other assets using a deed) stamp duty is payable at one per cent of the capital value of the property transferred, payable by the buyer. If you make a gift by deed, only 50p stamp duty is payable.

STAMP DUTY

We have had death duties in this country for centuries, but they keep changing their names, as Chancellors like to be seen to be reforming them. Until 1974 we had an Estate Duty, but then it became Capital Transfer Tax, only to be changed in 1984 back to Estate Duty, but this time called Inheritance Tax. The trouble is that many people, if they ever do write a will, leave it unreviewed for years - while politicians seem unable to leave the taxes that apply to wills alone. If you made a will some time ago - and you should have done - check if it is still appropriate.

Property can be handed on in two ways - by a lifetime gift (the jargon is still in Latin: *inter vivos*), or on death. Where are the tax problems?

DEATH DUTIES AND
WILLS

WHEN INHERITANCE TAX HAS TO BE PAID

Inheritance Tax (IHT) is payable on any transfer by an individual to another individual (or to a trust) which is not a market value transfer (ie part at least is a gift). It applies where that transfer happens either during the lifetime of the donor or on the donor's death. There are, however, some kinds of transfer exempt from the tax.

IHT does not apply to companies (except for anti-avoidance provisions aimed at small companies making gifts on behalf of individuals). It applies to gifts through settlements, but these are beyond the scope of this book.

THE AMOUNT OF IHT TO BE PAID

IHT works by adding up all the transfers within the scope of the tax, that is, all transfers made by the transferor in any seven-year period. The final period is the seven years before the donor's death, which are added with the total value of taxable property in the transferor's estate at death.

No IHT is payable up to a fixed total amount. Once the total of gifts in any seven-year period exceeds that amount, the lifetime rate of tax is payable. Once the total of the property in the estate and the gifts in the previous seven years exceeds that amount, tax is payable on the excess at the (higher) rate on death. A gift made in the period before the donor's death will become taxable at the higher rate although tax has been paid already at the lifetime rate. The current rates are given in the box opposite.

RATES OF INHERITANCE TAX: 1994-95

No tax is payable until the total of transfers reaches £150,000.

The lifetime rate for transfers over that sum is 20 per cent

Above that level, the higher rate is 40 per cent.

WHO PAYS IHT?

IHT payable on a lifetime gift is payable by the recipient out of the gift. The tax is, however, worked out on the basis that the total value of the gift is the actual gift plus the tax. For example, if you give away £8,000 taxable at the lifetime rate, the gift is treated as being £10,000 and the tax payable is £2,000. This is because the gift is treated as being the sum that, after deducting 20 per cent tax, leaves £8,000. In other words, the gift is the £8,000 plus the £2,000 tax.

IHT payable on an estate is paid by the executors or personal representatives, and it is their job to share the tax out among the beneficiaries. If there is a will, they must follow instructions in the will about who pays. This needs watching when writing a will. For instance, if Aunt Agatha wants to leave all her shares in Agatha's Cookies Ltd to nephew Neil, is he going to pay the IHT on the shares, or is someone else (and if so, who)? Can Neil afford to pay, or is he going to be forced to sell something to finance getting the shares? Should this be paid for by a life assurance policy bought by Agatha for the purpose?

IHT on the estate is payable out of the estate. So the tax on, say, the last £10,000 of the estate will be £4,000, leaving £6,000 to be passed to the beneficiaries of the estate.

IHT AND GIFTS

For IHT purposes, any large gift that is not exempt is a gamble. If the transferor dies within seven years of the date on which the gift is made, the value of the gift is added to the value of any property the transferor leaves on her or his death in calculating IHT liability. This does not apply to exempt gifts (see box). Even if tax has been paid at the 20 per cent rate, it will become taxable at the higher 40 per cent rate, so further tax will be due.

PLANNING FOR IHT

Points to watch in planning to reduce IHT liability:

While there is always a risk that there will be IHT to pay on a large gift, the younger the transferor the lower the risk

Make gifts of assets that are going to rise in value, and hang on to those that will not

It pays to use the exempt forms of transfer as far as appropriate, as there is no IHT on these

It may be wise to ensure that cash is available to pay any IHT that becomes due. A suitable life assurance policy made on the life of the donor in favour of the transferee may help

The form of the gift should be such as to reduce the amount of the gift for tax purposes (eg using exemptions)

Remember that although a transfer may be exempt from IHT, or the tax reduced, the gift will be separately taxable as a disposal of assets for CGT purposes. There may be stamp duty to pay. Each tax operates independently of the others.

GIFTS EXEMPTED FROM IHT

No IHT is payable on a lifetime transfer of any of the following kinds:

Transfers to the husband or wife of the transferor (unless he or she is based overseas).

There is also no CGT on these gifts. wedding gifts to children (up to £5,000), to grandchildren (up to £2,500) or others (up to £1,000)

The first £3000 a year of gifts by any transferor

Small gifts of £250 or less to any one recipient in any year

Gifts to charities. There is also no CGT on these gifts.

Gifts of heritage property (such as works of art of special value) approved by the Treasury. There is also no CGT on these gifts.

Gifts to political parties

Other gifts totalling in all less than the tax-free maximum amount (currently £15,000)

If the transferor dies more than three years after the date of the gift, but less than seven years later, the tax charge at the higher rate is reduced. The amount of the reduction is shown below:

Period between gift and death:	Percentage reduction of tax otherwise charged:
3-4 years	20 per cent
4-5 years	40 per cent
5-6 years	60 per cent
6-7 years	80 per cent

If, for example, the transferor dies 6 years and 6 months after making the gift, the amount of tax payable on the gift will be only one-fifth of that payable had the gift been made on death. Gifts within three years of death bear full tax at the higher rate.

Separately from the reliefs already mentioned, special reliefs operate to protect any gift or transfer of business property from the full rate of tax. If the transfer is of a business, or an interest in a business, full relief is given against the value of the property transferred. This means that the property entirely escapes tax. The same level of relief applies where the transfer is of shares giving the transferor control of a company running a business. It also applies to unquoted shares where the transferor did not have control but is transferring at least 25 per cent of the shares.

RELIEF ON TRANSFER
OF BUSINESS PROPERTY

In other cases, such as a smaller holding of shares, or assets held by a partnership of which the transferor is a partner, relief is only 50 per cent of the value.

Full relief is also available for transfers of **agricultural land** transferred with vacant possession. If the land is subject to a tenancy, the relief is 50 per cent.

DEATH AND TAXES

...as the saying goes, are the only two certainties. When someone dies, her or his estate must be transferred according to law to the beneficiaries. This amounts, in effect, to a disposal in the capital gains tax sense, but no capital gains tax is payable on a transfer of property on death. Instead, the beneficiaries are treated as receiving the property at its market value at the time of the death without any CGT being payable. There is also no stamp duty on transfers made because of a death.

Because of these exemptions, the only tax payable on death is IHT. This is payable, as we noted above, on the total value of both the estate and gifts made within the previous seven years. But some gifts are exempt when made on death.

LEGACIES EXEMPT FROM IHT

Property left on death is exempt in the following cases:

All transfers to the widow or widower
(unless based abroad), and

All transfers to charities, political parties or
of heritage property

The reliefs for business property also apply
to transfers on death

The beneficiaries on death are those people named in the will of the person who died, assuming he or she made a will (which should always be done). If no will has been made - and that is the case surprisingly often - the property is transferred under the intestacy rules laid down by law. Only if there is a will, can any systematic advantage be made of the IHT exemptions.

For IHT purposes, the value of the estate left on someone's death includes:

VALUING AN ESTATE

Everything that belongs to the person who
has died,
and

all property that comes into the estate because of the death

less

any debts, the cost of the funeral, and any reductions in the value of the estate caused by the death

Do you know what your estate would be worth, were anything to happen to you now? You might like to do a quick calculation. Add together:

(1) Your share in your home (is it jointly owned by both husband and wife, or just one of you);

(2) Your business or your share of it (noting that the value is reduced for IHT purposes by the business property relief - the business itself may go down in value when the owner dies if the business depends heavily on the personality of its owner because of loss of goodwill);

(3) Your bank and building society deposits, shares and other savings;

(4) Any other property or money of yours - for example the car;

(5) Any life policies that you took out and belong to the estate;

(6) Any damages due to the estate if, for example, your death was caused by a negligent motorist,

(7) Any insurance payments that might fall due on your death, for example on travel insurance or credit insurance.

From this take away all debts.

The answer probably suggests ...

Passing on your property to the family therefore involves a web of complications from income tax, capital gains tax, VAT, stamp duty and IHT. If you sell, there will be no IHT, and the buyer will pay the stamp duty. But it will make CGT harder to avoid if you are under 55. If you give it away now, you can postpone CGT and run a risk of IHT. If you leave it to pass after you die, there will be IHT, but CGT is avoided. We have now outlined the tax problems. Your task is to think through how best to put your own plans for retirement, and for protecting your business if you should die, into effect. The worst plan is no plan.

There should be several parts to your plan. First, get a proper will written for yourself, and review it from time to time. When you are younger, if married and bringing up children, the best will may be a simple one - just transferring the property to your husband or wife. But is that enough? What if, to think the unthinkable, your husband or wife (or anyone else to whom you leave something) dies at the same time as you, or just a little later? This could make two slices of tax payable (although there is tax relief to stop a full charge to tax where the same property passes on the death of two separate people in quick succession). If the transfer is to your husband or wife, the IHT exemption will fail to work. What reserve provisions do you need? It is that sort of problem that needs professional help - get in the experts.

We have largely ignored trusts in this book, but it is worth mentioning here that a trust may be an unavoidable answer if at your death the property must pass to your children, and they - or some of them - are under 18. A solicitor can advise on how to combine dealing with these various possibilities with the minimum IHT. There are tricky issues if, for example, your business as a sole trader has to be handed on to people too young to run it yet. The answer may be a trading trust - but who should the trustees be?

Another part to your planning should be lifetime transfers.

If you are happily married, it would be wise to make sure that your property is held between you in roughly equal shares. There is no tax of any kind on a transfer from husband to wife (or the other way round).

Should you start handing on part of the business to other members of the family, a bit at a time, now? The rules about exemptions, combined with the amount that can be transferred without paying tax, mean that considerable amounts of property can be transferred free of IHT. Generally, the first £3,000 every year is free of IHT, and you can transfer another £150,000 every seven years tax free. This is an average of a further £20,000 a year. It is not easy to transfer a business you own outright in bits to take advantage of this. It is easier if the business is owned by a company or, sometimes, if settlements are used. Or you can do it by taking out a life policy, making a gift of it to the family (so nothing comes into your estate on death), but continuing to pay the premiums yourself. Again, expert advice in this area will probably be wise.

11 *Business rates an land taxes*

I CAN'T REMEMBER who first said "Buy land - they don't make it any more". Does it matter? The advice is just as good whoever gave it. There's another truism that goes along with the first: "Tax land - they can't pretend it's not there." Much of our history reflects the way people have used those two pieces of advice. It's no wonder that we have several taxes on land and what we do with it. That's what this chapter is about - these taxes and the practical effect to you as an owner or user of land.

WHICH TAXES APPLY?

By far the most important is the **rates** - the **business rates**, and the **council tax** which replaced the poll tax. Rates are a tax on the occupation of land, and on the occupier rather than the owner. Apart from these local taxes, we also have

Income tax on income from land (Schedule A)

Capital gains tax on gains made from disposals of land

Inheritance tax if you make a gift of land

Stamp duty on the documents necessary to sell land or create leases, and

VAT on some supplies of use of land

THE TAX ON LAND
OCCUPATION

Rates are an annual charge payable to local councils (and used to finance local services). The rates charge is based on two factors:

The rateable value of premises, and

The rate poundage set for the year

The rates payable on any building are the amount produced by multiplying the rateable value of that building by the national business rate fixed for that year. If the rate is set at, say, £2 in the £, and the rateable value of a building is £3,000, the annual rate on the building is £6,000.

HOW RATEABLE
VALUE IS SET

It is the job of the local District Valuer's Office (DV) of the Inland Revenue to fix the rateable value (RV) of every building in its area. These values are entered on to a public list, along with short details of the basis of the valuation. Whenever considering buying or renting premises, make sure you check the RV from the sellers or landlords (unless the rates are included in the rent). If you have any queries, check with the local DV.

The DV sets the RV by reference to a notional rent for the building. It is the notional annual rent payable for those premises, and for their current use, by a tenant who has an annual tenancy from the owner of the building under which the tenant does the repairs. However, the DV only revalue buildings about every 15 years (unless something has changed) so RVs are often artificial. The most important point is the `tone of the list'. By this is meant the general level of RVs in the area around a particular property. The key question is whether the RV of the individual property compares correctly with those of its neighbours.

The comparison takes into account:

Rents actually being charged

The size of the building (to the nearest square metre)

Its use

Levels of profits

Local facilities

Local problems, such as double yellow lines preventing parking. It is the job of a surveyor who knows the area well to decide the correct RV for a property.

If you think an RV for premises you occupy is too

high, you can challenge it. To do this, ask the local DV for the necessary forms to get the RV reassessed. You will be asked to state an alternative RV, and give reasons why the present one is too high. It will often pay to get the experts in on this one. Choose a local professional surveyor to deal with the matter for you, and ask his advice. Before you do that, it may be useful to visit the local DV and ask one of the staff there to explain your RV, and tell them you think it too high. When I have done that, the staff were extremely helpful.

There is a formal procedure if you challenge an RV, which gives the DV time to make a counter-proposal. If you cannot reach agreement, the matter goes to a special local body known as the Local Valuation Court for an independent decision.

CHALLENGING AN RV

Business rates used to vary from one local council area to another. The rate is now fixed at national level. This has reduced variations from one town to the next significantly. However, the tax is now also national, so not all the local rates get spent locally.

THE NATIONAL BUSINESS RATE

Income tax on rents and other income from land is under **Schedule A,** which applies to all UK land. It charges tax on the profits made from the land each year, less expenses. It is not used to tax trades such as market gardening, farming, mining and quarries, fisheries, ferries, or piers that exploit land or buildings. These are all handled under the Schedule D rules set out in chapter 3. Schedule A is the landlord tax.

INCOME TAX ON RENTS

FURNISHED RENTS AND
SERVICE CHARGES

Schedule A applies <u>only</u> to land. This means for example that if you let a furnished flat, only part of the payment made by your tenant comes under these rules.

ALLOWABLE EXPENSES

If you impose a separate service charge it is not treated as rent. If you impose only one charge, eg, for renting a room, and the furniture in it, and as payment for services, the charge must be split between the various things it covers for tax purposes. The non-rent payments are either trading income, or are treated the same way (so the deductions rules, loss rules, etc are those covered in Chapters 3 and 5). This applies to **holiday lets** which are treated under special provisions just like trading income.

If you have income from a furnished let, you can tell the tax inspector that you want the whole lot treated under the non-land rules. This is worth doing if your expenses are greater than your income, so you can set the loss against any other similar income.

The only expenses deductible from rents received when working out the profit under the Schedule A rules are revenue expenses of approved kinds. Capital expenditure (for example, on improving a building) is not allowable. Instead it can be set off against the sale proceeds of the building for capital gains tax purposes. There are limited exceptions to this general rule, when capital allowances are available for expenditure on land or buildings. See Chapter 6.

The following revenue expenses may be deducted:

Maintenance and repairs costs (but not costs of improvements)

Buildings insurance premiums

Management expenses (eg on collecting rents or legal fees for a new tenancy agreement)

Rates and water rates, when paid by the landlord

Rent charges, ground or other rent paid by the landlord

Expenses incurred in providing services to tenants under leases for which they make no separate rent payment (eg maintaining the garden without separate cost to tenants)

If levying a service charge, you can deduct any of the forms of expenditure mentioned in Chapter 5, provided that the expense is incurred for the purpose of earnings the profits on that business. If you are letting furnished property, one deduction that is claimable is a reasonable allowance for wear and tear on the furniture.

FURNISHED HOLIDAY LETS

Technically, running furnished holiday lettings is not a business. The income is charged partly under Schedule A and partly under the parallel rules of Schedule D Case VI that apply to furnished lets instead of the trading income rules. To avoid injustice, a person whose income comes from holiday lettings is treated as if he or she is trading so as to claim tax reliefs, such as the CGT relief when retiring.

RENT OR BUY?

The tax rules may make some difference to the decision whether you rent premises for your business or buy them. If you rent, the full cost of the rent is a deductible expense for income tax purposes. If you buy, you can claim deduction for interest payments on the money borrowed (if any) to make the purchase. You can also sometimes claim capital allowances. The **post-tax** cost is worth checking - although it must be weighed against other factors such as the likely increase in property prices and/or rents in the area.

HOW THE TAX IS
PAYABLE

Income tax on rents is collected each year on the profits of that year's rents (unlike business income that is charged on the previous year's profits). That poses a practical problem. At the time the tax is payable, you probably don't know what the profits will be. The rules get out of that one by providing that you pay tax at first on the assumption that your profits this year will be the same as those last year. The tax bill will then be adjusted at the end of the year when the actual profit is known.

If you know the income this year is going to be down on last year's, notify the tax inspector, giving details of the new lower rents. If you do so, the tax office will adjust the tax bill without waiting to the end of the year.

STAMP DUTY ON
BUYING AND SELLING
LAND

If you buy or sell land, you have to use a formal document (called a deed of conveyance). If you do not use the proper formal document, the sale will be invalid. That's a good excuse for the government to impose a tax on the document, and they have done so for several hundred years. The duty is payable by the buyer.

A stamp duty is the tax you pay to have an official stamp put on your deed of conveyance. If you do not get the stamp put on the document, you cannot use the document in court - that is, you cannot enforce your rights under it. Consequently, you would be foolish not to pay the duty (as well as being liable to penalties). The stamp is put on the document by the Stamp Office of the Inland Revenue. If, as is usual, a solicitor or licensed conveyancer does the legal work for you on a purchase, it is his or her job to see this is done.

HOW MUCH IS THE
STAMP DUTY?

There is no stamp duty if the total price for selling the land is under £60,000. If the price is £60,000 or more, the duty is one per cent of the total price. The stamp is payable on the price of the land, not necessarily the total price. For example, if you are buying an office complete with full carpets, furnishings and equipment, you should pay stamp duty only on the price of the office, not the additional items. Therefore get the price split between the amount on the land, and the amount on other items. It is not worth playing clever tricks to avoid duty, for example by buying the land in several lots each costing £50,000. There are rules to prevent avoiding the duty in that way.

GIFTS OF LAND

If you make a gift of land, eg transferring the ownership of the building where the family business is carried on to your children, you may have to pay inheritance tax if you die within seven years after the gift. There may also be CGT on the gift. These have been discussed in other chapters. The stamp duty on a gift of land is 50p.

STAMP DUTY ON
RENTING PREMISES

Duty is payable on any lease or agreement to lease land. It is usual to have two copies of the document - one for the landlord to keep and the other (a duplicate) for the tenant. The full stamp duty is paid on the original copy, and a fee of 50p on the duplicate.

The amount of stamp duty on a lease depends on the length of the lease, the amount of any premium or capital sum payable, and the amount of any rent. If the tenancy is for less than a year (and one year less one day is quite commonly used), and the rent is over £600, the duty is one per cent (nothing if below £600). For longer periods the amount is based on both the rent and the premium.

VAT ON SUPPLIES OF
LAND AND BUILDINGS

There is no VAT chargeable on private sales of land or agreements allowing use of land. Where the supply is by a business, there may be VAT. Where a builder sells a commercial building he has built, there is VAT. If the sale is of a private house, the supply is zero-rated. The landlord may choose whether there is VAT on the rent of a leased commercial building.

Most other forms of supply of land (eg sale of land or of an older building, or grant of a tenancy of an older building) are exempt from VAT.

The following are always taxable:

Providing accommodation in a hotel, boarding house or somewhere similar;

Providing holiday accommodation;

Granting rights to camp, park, shoot, fish, moor a boat, mount an exhibition or play sports, or similar activities

These rules mean in effect that those using land for a trade (eg running a car park or holiday camp) have to charge VAT, but most others do not.

12   *When to pay... and not to pay*

WHEN YOU PAY TAX is often as important as how much you pay. Your planning should take account of both. It helps you watch your cash flow if you take full account of the timing of tax payments and allowances. As you will expect by now, there is no consistent set of rules about this for all taxes. We must also look at how the tax authorities decide how much is to be paid, and your rights to object. That's what we cover in this chapter.

HOW YOU PAY TAXES

There are three ways that tax is collected :

By deduction at source - the person making the payment is either entitled or required to deduct tax when making the payment, so that the person receiving the payment has already lost the tax from it

By transaction taxes - dealt with at the time of a particular transaction with the items taxed, for example, when they are sold

By annual taxes - or other taxes collected over a period, where the amount of tax will depend on, for example, the profits over a period. In these cases taxes have to be collected after the period is over, although there may be some sort of provisional advance payment

This method of collecting tax is used as widely as possible by both the Inland Revenue and the DSS. The following kinds of income are subject to a requirement or entitlement for the payer to collect tax on their behalf :

DEDUCTING AT SOURCE

Earnings from employment.
Employers must operate PAYE on all taxable earnings, to collect income tax due from the employee, and Class 1 contributions due to the NI Fund from both employer and employee. Employers must also pay the Class 1A contributions on cars in this manner. The tax and NI contributions must be worked out and deducted every time payment is made to an employee, so that the employee only receives pay after deductions. The tax and NI contributions collected in this way must be paid to the Revenue within 14 days after the end of each tax month.

Bank, building society and other interest.
Banks and societies pay interest on all smaller deposits (less than £50,000) after taking off income tax. They pay the tax due direct to the Revenue. This is also true of yearly interest due from the government, local authorities or companies on most bonds

and debentures. However, some bonds are exempt and can also be set up.

Company dividends and distributions. Companies strictly do not deduct tax at source from dividends. Instead they pay ACT (advance corporation tax) to the Revenue at the same time. In practical terms, this amounts to the same thing from the viewpoint of an individual shareholder, though a company shareholder is protected from tax on dividends. ACT is based on three-month periods, the Revenue being paid at the end of the three-month period the amount of ACT due during that period less any tax credits received from other companies during that period. Tax is paid at the same time regardless of when during the three months the dividend is paid.

Covenants and annual payments.
Making payments by covenant used to be a widespread way of saving tax. The present tax system largely ignores them, except when the person receiving the money is a charity. Payment to a charity by a four-year covenant is still a good idea for a business but is complicated by deduction at source. Most big charities have standard forms of covenant to use and leaflets explaining how the tax relief works. If in doubt, contact the Charities Aid Foundation. Businesses can also give money through Gift Aid. This allows tax deduction for one-off charity gifts. But there is a minimum of £400 to claim tax relief.

The most important of these is VAT. Besides the question of what is subject to VAT and what is not, watch also when VAT is collected from customers, paid to suppliers, and accounted for to the VAT Office. If you monitor this carefully, it could help your cash flow considerably. In smaller businesses, it may also improve your cash flow if you are on the cash accounting scheme. The annual VAT accounting scheme is of considerable help to smaller businesses - though it won't allow you to put off paying for a year. Instead, you are asked to pay tax in 10 instalments with the final instalment being used to get the amount of VAT right for the year. Any business may ask to pay in this way if its turnover is below £300,000 and its VAT affairs are in order.

VAT is, for most businesses, dealt with on a three-monthly accounts basis, the tax due to the VAT Office being payable within a month from the end of the three-month period. There are stiff penalties, which will be readily imposed, if you fail to pay at the right time, so do not pay late - it will cost you a lot more.

Because of the three-monthly periods, it is worthwhile for a business trying to collect any VAT on outputs earlier rather than later during the three-month period, with the reverse applying to VAT paid out on inputs. For instance, if you have a number of large bills bearing VAT, get them paid at the beginning of a VAT accounting period, and you can keep the VAT in a deposit account for a few months before you pay it over. By contrast, if you are buying an expensive item, do so near the end of the three-month period and the gap between paying the VAT and getting it back will be reduced as far as may be.

TAXES ON
TRANSACTIONS

Is the business accounting on a cash basis ? If it is on an earnings basis, you must account for the VAT on the bills you send out, not the cash you collect. If your customers are slow payers, you may be paying out VAT to the VAT Office before getting it from the customer. In these cases smaller businesses should get themselves on to the cash accounting scheme. This will help your cash flow. If you are making mainly zero-rated supplies and are regularly claiming tax back, you should ask to be put on to a monthly return so you are not out of pocket.

VAT on imports, and **Customs Duty**, has to be paid when the goods are brought in, unless you use a freeport. **Excise Duties**, such as tobacco tax, are normally paid as the goods on which the duty falls are released from a bonded warehouse for onward sale or supply. This applies whether the goods are imports or domestic products.

THE ANNUAL TAXES

Taxes on profits have to be charged over a period - this applies to income tax, corporation tax, capital gains tax, and NI contributions on the self-employed. Of course, because of PAYE and the other deductions at source, the government gets a lot of this tax when the income is paid but some forms of income are only taxable afterwards.

TRADING AND PROFESSIONAL INCOME AND INCOME TAX

Tax payable under Schedule D Cases I and II on trading and professional income is payable in two instalments. The first half is due on 1 January. in the tax year for which it is payable, and the other half is due on 1 July after that tax year. As this tax is usually based on the **preceding year basis**, this means, for example that tax for the year 1994-95 will be due on 1 January 1995 and 1 July 1995. Under the rules explained above, this will usually be based on the accounts year ending in 1993-94. As we saw, this rule will have changed by 1997.

From the point of view of cashflow you pay tax on these dates and get the benefit of allowances then regardless of when the profits were earned or the allowances gained. It therefore pays to receive income earlier rather than later in the year, but to meet expenditure which qualifies for allowances later rather than earlier. You can in some cases increase or decrease the gap between getting and paying, or spending and paying, by nearly 12 months. It's better in a lot of cases to spend money near the end of your accounts year, rather than a month later. You get the tax relief a whole year earlier.

OTHER INCOME TAX
PAYMENTS

Basic rate income tax is payable on any other kind of taxable income on 1 January in the tax year for which it is payable. In most cases the tax is based on that year's income (though there are special rules about land taxation).

HIGHER RATE
INCOME TAX

Payment of tax due at the higher rate of tax (taking account of tax already paid at the basic rate) is due later than the basic rate tax - on 1 December after the tax year for which it is collected. It is payable shortly before the second instalment of tax on trading income, but after payment of any other basic rate tax. Higher rate tax for 1994-95 is therefore due on 1 December.

NI CONTRIBUTIONS

Class 1 contributions are payable under the PAYE scheme. Class 2 contributions are payable by banker's order every month. Class 4 contributions are paid at the same time as the trading income taxation, on 1 January and 1 July.

CAPITAL GAINS TAX

CGT payments by individuals are made at the same time as higher rate income tax -1 December after the end of the tax year for which the payment is made. It may be of advantage to time sales giving rise to taxable gains early in the tax year, and those giving rise to losses late in the tax year, so as to increase the cashflow where possible.

Two other points to watch on CGT are :

To spread capital gains so that you use the annual allowance of tax-free gains. If you do not use this in a year, you cannot carry it forward to the next.

If you have made a loss, cash it in so that you cancel out gains. You can do this by selling assets such as shares at their market value, and then buying the equivalent back again - also at market value. If you have made a loss, you can set it off against CGT payable on gains on other sales. As with trading income, it is worth watching what year things occur in.

CORPORATION TAX

As already noted, ACT has to be paid on three-monthly accounts following the period in which a distribution is paid out. The ACT, as its name indicates, is treated as an advance payment of the corporation tax due. Any other tax due (called the mainstream corporation tax) is payable nine months after the end of the accounting period of the company for which the tax is being paid. So, if the company uses an annual calendar year, the tax is payable at the end of the following September. For most small companies, however, the ACT will meet all or most of their mainstream corporation tax bill, because ACT is now collected at the same rate as the small companies' rate of corporation tax. See Chapter 7.

INHERITANCE TAX

IHT is payable during the course of winding up the estate of the deceased. In practice, the IHT has to be calculated and paid by the personal representatives of the deceased (or their solicitors) when applying for the formal grant of probate or letters of administration (that is, the formal court authority to deal with the property left by the person who died). Where tax becomes payable on a gift made within 7 years of the death because of the death, the tax is due six months after the end of the month in which the person died.

PAYING LATE : THE PENALTIES

Unless there is a dispute as a result of which late payment of tax is approved, paying tax late is likely to land the taxpayer with a demand for interest on the sums overdue, penalties, or both.

INTEREST ON LATE TAX

Where a payment of any of the taxes collected by the Inland Revenue - income tax, CT, CGT, IHT - is late, interest is payable by the taxpayer on the amount overdue from the date payment should have been made. This is chargeable both where a bill for tax has not been met, and also where for some reason the Revenue are recovering back tax (for example, they only discover that someone is trading several years after they started). The interest is treated and collected as part of the tax bill, and is not an allowable expense. The Revenue do not usually collect interest of less than £50. Above that sum, the Revenue computer will calculate and mail you a bill with, you may feel, excessive efficiency if you are inefficient. The rate of interest at the time of writing is 5 per cent. This is varied from time to time. It is not deductible as an expense against other tax!

The interest payments for late tax also apply to late payments of NI contributions collected by the Revenue. In other cases, there is a hidden interest rate for late NI payments (for example, Class 2) because you have to pay at the current weekly rate, not the previous one.

PENALTIES FOR LATE TAX

Penalties for late payment - or incorrect payment - of VAT are tough. If a return is not made in time (and therefore the VAT due with the return is not paid), the VAT Office can impose an assessment on the taxpayer. When that happens, a default surcharge can be levied on the taxpayer. Interest is also payable.

REPAYMENT SUPPLEMENTS

If you have overpaid tax the authorities must return it and make a **repayment supplement**. This is interest payable to you on the tax overpaid. For some taxes it is not payable unless the tax has been overpaid for more than 12 months after the end of the tax year for which it was paid, and only then if it exceeds £30. The interest rate is the same as that which taxpayers must pay the tax authorities. Repayment supplements are payable by both the Inland Revenue and Customs and Excise.

Most of you no doubt think this is the topic to start with, not to end with. Well ... it is and it isn't. What we need to do at the end is to sum up tax planning points made in the book. We also need to look at how the amount of tax is decided in individual cases, and how tax disputes are sorted out.

WHEN NOT TO PAY

There are three key aspects of tax planning which we now need to tie together:

TAX PLANNING :
A SUMMARY

Pay no more tax than you need. If you can take proper, and commercially sensible, action to cut your tax bill, it is your right to do so. Indeed, you will be expected to do so. Do so within the tax laws, taking full advantage of them.

Get your timing right. Watch your cash flow and plan for the effects of tax. If you can so arrange things within the rules that you owe the tax authorities money, rather than them owing it to you, you are entitled to do so.

Don't go over the top. Compared with a few years ago, two aspects of tax planning have fundamentally changed. First, no one tax rate is now over 40 per cent. Gone are the days of crippling tax rates when it was better to do anything rather than pay. When planning, get things in proportion. Second, Parliament and the courts have made it a lot harder to get up to `clever' avoidance tricks to cut tax bills through complex schemes. There are a whole range of complicated provisions designed to reduce the extent to which people can avoid tax in situations where Parliament or the courts have decided that it would be wrong to do so.

Remember that where a tax avoidance scheme involves **several stages** or steps sorted out in advance, some of which are there just to avoid tax, the courts will simply **ignore** what has been done, and look at what has gone on behind the scenes. For example, if Al sells shares to Mig, in order that Mig sells them to Zale (rather than Al selling them direct to Zale) the courts may say that this is really a sale straight from Al to Zale if the only reason for Mig getting involved was to avoid tax.

THINGS TO THINK ABOUT

Take all the taxes into account when planning

Check when tax is payable as well as how much

You now pay the same tax rates on income and on capital gains

Trading accounts need adjusting for tax purposes

It is for you to show you are entitled to deductions - they aren't granted automatically

Work out if you should trade through a company or direct

Don't just buy - check if you are better off leasing equipment or renting premises

When selling assets, get your timing right

Pay yourself and your staff in the best way

Claim full reliefs for any losses

Sort VAT out before it sorts you out

Make sure your business plans take full account of your rights to grants and incentives

Don't leave planning for the future to the future. Both for the sake of your business and your family, plan ahead for retirement

RETURNS AND
ASSESSMENTS

Tax authorities rely on accurate and timely information to check everyone is paying the right amounts of tax. To get this information, they have extensive powers to demand **returns**. You are required to make returns each year setting out your full income, so that your income tax bill can be worked out. You will also be involved in other returns: PAYE returns on tax collected from employees, P11D returns on higher-paid staff, returns on any company profits, and on any dividends or interest paid by the company, forms to sort out your NI liability, and VAT returns - plus returns when inheritance tax or stamp duty is payable.

When the returns have been sent in, officials use them to calculate what tax is due and then issue **assessments** for the tax payable. The formal assessment is a statement of what is due and when it is payable. This is necessary every year to tax trading and professional income and any taxable gains. However, we are steadily moving to **self-assessment**. Corporation tax is now collected through **Pay and File**. By 1997 something similar will have taken effect for income tax too. Assessments are then kept, as with VAT, for defaulters or in cases where the tax authorities do not accept the returns made.

MORE PENALTIES

If a taxpayer fails to make a return when asked, or fails to disclose taxable income or gains to the tax authorities, they have two powers to handle the problem. First, they can impose an estimated assessment on the taxpayer. Second, they can impose penalties for failing to answer the request for a return.

An **estimated assessment** is a tax officer's guess at the taxable income or gains for the period. If a trader fails to file a return of trading income or for VAT, tax officials will impose an estimated assessment of the profits of the business on her or him. If an estimated assessment is imposed on you, and you do not appeal, then you have to pay the tax due on that estimate. What happens on an appeal is set out below. It should not surprise if they guess high when imposing an estimate, especially if they have already done so before.

Penalty powers can be severe. For failing to make a return, it is £300 in the first instance. For failing to declare tax fully and correctly the maximum penalty is £300 plus the amount of tax lost (twice the amount of tax lost if the taxpayer is suspected of fraud), plus interest. What makes the powers severe is that they can be imposed for every year in which tax is underpaid - back to 1936. If a wayward taxpayer has failed, say, to pay £1,000 that should have been paid each year for the last ten years, the tax authorities will not only issue a tax bill for the £10,000, but also penalties and interest on both overdue tax and penalties. The resulting maximum penalty is severe.

VAT PENALTIES

These used to involve prosecutions, but have now been altered to be more in line with the Revenue's powers. The Revenue rarely prosecutes offenders if they pay up, whilst the VAT authorities have been more ready to do so. They have powers to impose - and will impose - penalties if your returns are late or do not have the correct amount of VAT attached to them. Again, if the tax has been understated, penalties attach to the demand for back tax.

Penalties also apply to failure to register when

this should be done - and tax that should have been collected will still be demanded.

DO YOU HAVE TAX APPEAL ?

If you do not agree with an assessment made on you, you have the right to appeal to an independent appeal tribunal. But watch two points. It is up to you to prove your appeal, not the tax authorities. If they impose an estimated assessment on you, you can only succeed if you can show the tax appeal body that *on the balance of probabilities* the guess is wrong. If the tax inspector has just made a broad guess, and you have no records to show he is wrong, his guess will be upheld.

The second point is that you need to appeal fast. Your right of appeal against a tax assessment lasts 30 days. You appeal by writing back to the tax inspector or officer who imposed the assessment on you objecting to it, and giving an outline of the reasons. The assessment gives you details. Normally both you and the inspector will expect the matter to be settled. If they have put an estimated assessment on you, and you produce proper accounts, the correct assessment will be issued instead. If not, it will go before independent tax appeal commissioners (or the Value Added Tax Tribunal in the case of VAT). If your case is going that far, it's probably time to get the experts in.

PAST ERRORS : CLAIM NOW

We saw that the tax authorities can go back to open previous years' tax bills if something was left out. You have the same right if you have forgotten to claim something. If by reason of some error or mistake of yours in a return (such as not claiming a deduction for an allowable expense), you have paid too much tax to the Revenue, give written notice of it to your tax inspector. It can be corrected for a period of up to six years after the end of the year when the error was made. If something in this book has told you that you should have been claiming for relief, it may not be too late.

TAX WORDS

Note: this section contains explanations of many of the words in bold in the text of the book. Others are explained in full at the appropriate place in the text. To check those words, consult the index.

What do we mean by....

ACT (Advance Corporation Tax)
The tax paid by a company when it pays a dividend. The ACT goes direct to the Revenue, but the taxpayer gets a **tax certificate** for tax paid. The taxpayer can use this to avoid paying any further **basic rate** income tax on the dividend. At the same time, the company can use it to cancel out payment of **mainstream corporation tax.**

Allowable expenses
Expenses allowable for **Income Tax** or **Corporation Tax,** consisting of **CGT** expenses of kinds specifically allowed and not prohibited under the rules of each tax.

Anti-avoidance
Anti-avoidance rules are aimed at counteracting tax avoidance techniques. They can be broad provisions which have a very powerful effect, such as assuming that someone earned money that he has never received. These provisions are normally only used to counteract transactions which have no reason other than reducing or cutting out paying tax.

Assessment
Formal imposition of tax liability (applies to all taxes); also refers to the forms issued containing the assessment.

Asset
Term used, particularly in CGT, for any kind of property whatsoever, ie anything on which cash could be raised.

Assisted Areas
Areas designated by the government where a business can receive regional selective assistance.

Balancing allowance (and **Balancing charge**)
The adjustment increasing (or decreasing) the amount of capital allowance available to a taxpayer when disposing of a capital item on which an allowance has been made.

Basic rate
The main rate of income tax (the rate applying to over 90 per cent of taxpayers), as contrasted with the higher rate (since 1988 there is only one higher rate) payable on income over a set level.

Benefit in kind
Payment to an employee made other than in cash (often called perks), eg company car, cheap loan.

Business rate
Tax imposed on the occupation of business properties, payable to the local authority for local services.

Capital
For income tax purposes means receipts of expenditures which do not count as income or allowable expenses. See capital allowance, CGT.

Capital allowance
A deduction against income or corporation tax in respect of capital expenditure.
Cash basis
Drawing up accounts on the basis that entries are only made when

cash is received or paid out, not when income is earned.

CGT
Capital gains tax - the tax payable by individuals who make a chargeable gain on the disposal of assets.

Chargeable gain
That part of a capital gain liable to CGT.

Charging section
A section of a Finance Act which directly imposes a tax.

Compliance
The description given by accountants to work done to ensure their clients comply with the requirements of tax authorities.

Contracted-out
Usually refers to contracted-out occupational pension schemes whose members are not entitled to the earnings-related supplement to the retirement pension, and who pay lower contracted-out rates of Class 1 NICs. Also refers to individuals who contract out using a personal pension plan.

Contributions Agency
The executive agency of the DSS responsible for collecting NI contributions.

Corporation Tax
Tax payable by companies (and certain societies and clubs) on their income and chargeable gains in place of income tax and capital gains tax.

Council Tax
Tax payable to local councils by local residents. Each house is given a "band" and the tax is levied at a set amount for each band in each council area.

Covenant
Gift made by deed promising annual payments - usually lasting for a minimum of four years to a charity - because otherwise they don't work for tax purposes. Covenants in favour of individuals will not work after 16 March 1988 unless made before then, that is, they

make no difference to the tax position of the covenantor or the recipient.

Customs and Excise
The government department responsible for collecting customs and excise duties and VAT.

Customs duty
Protective duties imposed by the European Community at its frontiers to protect products made within the Community from excessive outside competition. Similarly, other states impose customs duties on imports from Community countries including the UK.

Disposal
Technical term in CGT for getting rid of an asset whether by sale, gift, exchange or any other means (including losing it).

Double taxation
When something either gets caught by two different taxes, or (usually) by taxes of two different countries.

DSS
The Department of Social Security. This is the department responsible for collecting National Insurance contributions and paying social security benefits.

Earnings basis
Drawing up accounts on the basis that entries are made when income is earned and when bills are incurred (compare cash basis).

Enterprise allowance
Weekly allowance from the government for those who were unemployed and are starting out in self-employment.

Enterprise zone
Area designated by the government as eligible for special tax breaks.
European Community or European Union
The (at present) 12 states comprising UK together with Belgium, Denmark, France, West Germany, Greece, Ireland, Luxembourg, the Netherlands, Italy, Portugal and Spain. The EC or EU (for short) is the tax authority for customs duties and agricultural levies within the

12 member states, rather than the states themselves. The term European Union arises from the Treaty of European Union (usually called the Maastricht Treaty) which came into effect in 1994.

Evasion
Illegal measures designed to remove, reduce or postpone the payment of tax.

Excise duties
Taxes imposed upon specific goods usually at the production or input state, particularly tobacco, alcoholic drinks and petrol.

Exempt
Prevented from being taxed by a specific rule. For example, an exempt asset for CGT purposes is an asset for which no CGT is due if there is a disposal; the exempt amount is the annual allowance for CGT before tax is payable on gains; an exempt supply for VAT purposes is a supply on which the supplier must not charge VAT.

Finance Act
Name given to the law which each year (sometimes twice) imposes that year's tax rates and changes (eg Finance Act 1994).

Financial year
The year from 1 April to 31 March over which corporation tax is imposed and levied, and which is the Government's accounting year.

Freeport
One of the areas designated by the Government in which customs duty and VAT do not have to be paid until goods leave the port.

Gain
Any realised increase in value of an asset for CGT, on which the tax will be imposed; more generally any increase in value or wealth (same as profit).

Gift
Payment (in cash or kind) made to someone else voluntarily without any contract or payment back. Does not count as income for income tax purposes unless made by covenant, but may get caught by inheritance tax and CGT.

Higher paid employee
Old term for employee earning £8,500 or more a year, for whom special rules on benefits in kind apply. (Description abolished in 1989.)

IHT (**Inheritance tax**) (see below).

Income
Has several meanings. The widest is anything which comes in, or any increase in a person's wealth over a period, less her or his expenditure. As in income tax, it means those kinds of receipt which are taxable under the charging sections of income tax.

Income tax
Tax payable by individuals, partners and trusts (but not companies) on some kinds of income (and some things that are not income). What is 'income' for these purposes is nowhere defined. Instead, income tax catches forms of payments received which fall under any one of the separate charging sections known as Schedules and Cases. These are:

Schedule A	Tax on rents and other receipts from land and buildings in the UK
Schedule B	Doesn't exist any longer
Schedule C	Tax on income from Government bonds

Schedule D

Case I	Tax on trades
Case II	Tax on professions and vacations
Case III	Tax on interest,annual payments, discounts
Case IV	Tax on interest and other income from securities held overseas
Case V	Tax on any other form of overseas income aside from overseas earnings
Case VI	Tax on things left out elsewhere such as furnished lettings, occasional earnings of a professional kind (eg from one article in a magazine), and anti-avoidance provisions
Schedule E	Tax on earnings from employments, pensions, and social security payments
Schedule F	Tax on payments from UK companies of dividends and other forms of distribution

Income tax year
The year running from 6 April to 5 April over which income tax is imposed and levied each year.

Indexation allowance
The adjustment to be made to any allowable expenditure against a gain for CGT to reflect the rise in prices between buying the asset and disposing of it.

Industrial buildings
The only buildings (special industries aside) for which capital allowances are available.

Inheritance tax
The tax payable on someone's death in connection with property left by that person on his death, or gifts made within seven years before death or certain payments made through settlements in that period.

The government department in charge of our direct taxes: income tax, CGT, corporation tax, stamp duty, inheritance tax.

Input tax
VAT paid by a taxpayer on inputs to the business, that is, supplies made to the taxpayer. Deductible from output tax.

Inspector of Taxes
The local representative of the Inland Revenue, responsible for income tax, CGT and corporation tax for an area known as a **district**.

IRC
Inland Revenue Commissioners (or Board of Inland Revenue, which is the same people). There is no minister directly in charge of the Inland Revenue, so the Commissioners are in charge instead.

Loss relief
Method of providing an offset for a loss against taxable income (for income tax or corporation tax) or chargeable gains (for CGT).

Mainstream Corporation Tax
The corporation tax due from a company nine months after the end of any accounting year in respect of the profits of that year.

Moonlighting
Doing a second job of which the tax authorities are not aware.

NIC   National Insurance Contributions
The name usually (but technically incorrectly) given to the contributions payable under the Social Security Acts in respect of the cost of financing the state's pension funds. They are divided into four classes:

Class 1   contributions payable by both employee and employer on the earnings of the employee

Class 2   flat-rate weekly amount payable by anyone who is self-employed

Class 3   voluntary flat-rate weekly sum that may be paid by those not required or entitled to pay contributions under Classes 1 or 2

Class 4   contributions payable by those traders and

Class 4   contributions payable by those traders and professionals paying tax under income tax Schedule D Cases I and II

Output tax
VAT imposed on outputs, that is, supplies made by the taxpayer.

PAYE
Pay As You Earn, the scheme under which employers have to collect income tax and Class 1 NICs from employees' pay before it is paid.

P11D
Form used to report non-cash earnings of higher paid employees and directors.

Personal allowances   The tax-free amounts granted to all individuals before income tax is levied on a year's taxable income.

Personal pension
The scheme for non-state retirement pensions introduced in 1988 which can be purchased (with available income tax relief) by anyone.

Plant and machinery
Official language used to describe business equipment on which capital allowances are available.

Post-tax
Looking at something after taking into account the tax payable (for example, the post-tax cost of a deductible expense is less than it costs you in cash terms).

Preceding year basis
The rule whereby income tax on trading income is normally charged on the income not of the year of charge but of the previous year.

Profit
Has several meanings, as do gain and income; can mean all receipts from something (gross profits); or all income less expenses (net profits); or revenue receipts liable to income tax (annual profits).

Rateable value
Value put on a property so that anyone occupying it can be charged rates, based on notional annual rental value.

Rates
The tax payable to a local council by businesses occupying land or buildings within the area of the local authority.

Regional selective assistance
Name given to the power of the Department of Trade and Industry, Scottish Office and Welsh Office to issue grants to assist industries to create or protect employment in the assisted areas.

Rollover relief
Relief from CGT when tax due under the tax can be postponed, or rolled over, if the taxpayer carries out some action (eg spending the gain on replacement assets).

Stamp duty
Tax paid for a stamp (usually stamped in the old sense) placed on documents, without which the documents are not fully valid; currently required on most conveyances, leases and transfers of shares, but to be abolished on share transactions late in 1991-92.

Standard rate
The main rate of VAT; also the main rate of Class 1 NICs (compare the basic rate of income tax).

Supply
Name given to a transaction on which VAT must be imposed - the transfer of ownership of goods or the rendering of services whether or not for a price.

Tax avoidance
Any legal steps to remove, reduce, or postpone tax payments (as compared with evasion).

Tax break
An opportunity to reduce your tax bill - also tax shelter, an Americanism used to refer to anything which will shelter your income or capital from tax, ie can be used to offset and reduce your

tax bill.

Tax certificate
Or certificate of deduction, shows that tax has been deducted at source on a payment, or that ACT has been paid on a dividend; used by the recipient to claim a tax credit.

Tax credit
Credit against tax due from a taxpayer because tax has been collected or paid by someone else (eg on a dividend).

Tax haven
A country where tax is levied at a lower rate or not at all.

Tax invoice
Invoice or bill that must be issued for VAT purposes by a taxpayer imposing VAT on supplies to another VAT taxpayer.

Tax point
Time when VAT becomes payable on a supply.

Taxable income
That amount of a person's income which is liable to income tax under the income tax schedules and cases.

VAT
Value added tax. This is the tax payable when anyone makes a supply of goods or services in the course or furtherance of any economic activity carried on by the supplier, unless it is an exempt supply.

Year of assessment
The technical name of the income tax year.

Zero rate
A nil rate of tax - used in VAT to allow a supplier to recover the input tax whilst charging no output tax.

Index